A Ghost Hunter's Guide to

The Most Haunted Places

In America

Terrance Zepke

WHAT REVIEWERS ARE SAYING ABOUT ZEPKE'S MOST HAUNTED SERIES...

"One of the things I really like about Terrance's book is that it is such an easy read. The tidbits of history keep you turning the pages, and you also learn about the paranormal investigators, who have used a variety of paranormal investigation tools...*A Ghost Hunter's Guide to The Most Haunted Places in America* is one of those books that keeps your imagination wondering what really happened."
-Josh Schubert, **USA Travel Magazine**

"...*A Ghost Hunter's Guide To The Most Haunted Places in America*" explores the story behind these ghost story settings all throughout the country, from theatres, old factories, asylums, homes prisons, and much more. A Ghost Hunter's Guide to The Most Haunted Places in America is a must for lovers of the paranormal in America. Highly recommended.
-James A. Cox, **Midwest Book Review**

"From a lunatic asylum to a brewery, ghostly presences inhabit all these places. Complete directions and site information is provided. Even if you don't get a chance to visit each of these locations, the stories and the black-and-white photos are fascinating.
-Marcella Gauthier, **Escapees Magazine**

"You don't have to believe in ghosts to realize that certain places in our national history are haunted with legends and spirits of long ago. Terrance Zepke grew up in South Carolina knowing the tales of colonial pirates, Civil War legends, the impact of lowcountry voodoo, and the famous residents of weathered cemeteries…places you probably best not visit at night, She's written books such as *Coastal South Carolina: Welcome to the Lowcountry, Best Ghost Tales of South Carolina, Pirates of the Carolinas*, and her latest book, *A Ghost Hunter's Guide to the Most Haunted Places in America*, investigates saloons and cemeteries, former sanitariums, and penitentiaries across America where rumors of strange phenomenon seem to have some bearing…Terrance is one of the most schooled experts on paranormal in the United States."

–Rick Steves, ***Travel with Rick Steves***

"…From Georgia to California, Terrance writes about places that are home to a ghost or two -- and tells the horrible tales that led to these creatures remaining close to where they died. Her first chapter is about the Trans-Allegheny Lunatic Asylum in West Virginia, the place that creeped her out the most in her investigations into the paranormal -- and the one closest to where I live. It is told that many of the poor souls who died in the facility -- often from experimental treatments and procedures -- continue to roam the halls. Yawsa."

-Teresa Flatley, ***BoomThis! Magazine***

"…Zepke herself has always loved a good ghost story and heard many as she was growing up in the Carolinas. Now she has many books recording not only the stories she loves but also the history and photos of the places named. These places have all been investigated and proven haunted by the most sophisticated modern scientific equipment such as EMF detectors, which register electrical and magnetic fields, and EVP's (Electronic Voice Phenomenon), which digitally records sounds the human ear cannot detect. Each place Zepke writes about has all the tour contact information also and many black and white photos. A fun way to plan a trip, if you aren't afraid!"

-Bonny Neely (**Top 1,000 Amazon Reviewer**)

"…a journalist by training, she [Zepke] takes you on a tour of the Trans-Allegheny Lunatic Asylum in West Virginia, the Birdcage Theatre in Arizona, and the Colonial Park Cemetery in Georgia, among a dozen other places…"

-Alan Caruba, **Bookviews.com** (National Book Critics Circle)

ISBN-10: 0985539801

ISBN-13: 978-0-9855398-0-1

Cover design by Michael Swing.

Safari Publishing

Inquiries should be addressed to: www.safaripublishing.net
For more about the author: www.terrancezepke.com

1.Ghosts. 2. Paranormal. 3. Hauntings-America. 4. American Folklore-Ghosts. 5. Ghost Investigations/Tours. 6. Haunted Attractions. I. Title.

Second Edition
Printed in the U.S.A.

Terrance Zepke

A Ghost Hunter's Guide to The Most Haunted Places in America

About the Author

Terrance Zepke loves ghost stories and travel. She has lived and traveled all over the world during her career as an adventure travel writer. She has explored every continent and enjoyed all kinds of adventures—from dog-sledding in the Arctic to surviving an overnight stay in an extremely haunted lunatic asylum. Even though she has lived in exciting cities, such as Honolulu and London, she calls the Carolinas her "true home." She can't decide which state she likes best so she divides her time between North and South Carolina. She grew up in the South Carolina Lowcountry, which is what ignited her interest in ghosts. The Lowcountry is full of haunted places and tales of boo hags, hoodoo, and haints. Terrance has written numerous books on the history and folklore of the Carolinas, as well as dozens of travel guides (See the last page of this book for a list of all titles).

Introduction

As the author of numerous ghost books, I have been asked a lot of questions about ghostly phenomenon over the years, including some really strange questions. But the most common query I get is something that you may be wondering too, *"How and why did you start writing ghost books?"*

There are two reasons. First, I love a good ghost story. After all, I grew up in the South Carolina Lowcountry where storytelling and haunted plantations and things like ghosts and boo hags are as much a way of life as iced tea and humidity. Since I'm a writer and I love a good ghost story, it was inevitable that I would write about ghosts. I love to share a good ghost tale!

The longer reason is the research. In order to understand who or rather what entity haunts a place, you have to know the backstory. This means you have to put together a detailed history about a place.

There is nothing I enjoy more than learning about how a historic house or hotel or asylum or prison came to be built, who inhabited it, and what happened to the inhabitants. The research proves especially intriguing in regards to what kind of paranormal activity has been detected and by whom and for how long and how recently.

Usually, places are haunted due to their rich history—murder, betrayal, love, greed, lust, war, disease, tragedy, death, duels, gambling disputes—and the list goes on. The theory is that spirits that died tragically may have unfinished business so they linger where they died.

For example, the Birdcage Theatre in Tombstone is believed to be haunted by many spirits, including a prostitute named Margarita who was killed by another prostitute known as Gold Dollar. A stagehand named "Red" haunts the Lincoln Theatre, a child named Lilly still plays at the Trans-Alleghany Lunatic Asylum, cowboys still roam the streets of Tombstone, Nina stalks the Shanghai Tunnels searching for her freedom, the spirit of Pearl Bryan haunts Bobby Mackey's Music World after being violently murdered (and beheaded), no telling how many men who were shanghaied onto pirate ships still linger in The Pirates' House, inmates who endured "the hole" and the "iron gag" remain incarcerated at Eastern State Penitentiary, the spirit of legendary Voodoo Priestess Marie Laveau haunts the cemetery where she was buried in New Orleans, a man named James Jones Stark who was killed during a duel harasses patrons and employees of the Moon River Brewing Company, and one psychic claims there are as many as 600 ghosts on board the *Queen Mary*.

In each of the chapters, I have included the results of various ghost investigations whenever possible. Scientific results go a lot farther in substantiating supernatural activity than anything a witness can say or feel. As most of you are aware, ghost investigators bring all kinds of technical equipment that help prove or disprove paranormal activity, such as EMF detectors. These detect electrical and magnetic fields. Electronic Voice Phenomenon or EVPs are another way to determine if a place is haunted. A digital recorder records sounds that the human ear cannot detect. There are lots of other good tools, including motion detectors and thermal cameras, which pick up changes in the temperature. These things help rule out other possibilities, such as hoaxes or reflections or silhouettes. All the places discussed in this publication have lots of evidence supporting the claims of being haunted.

I hope you like reading this book as much as I enjoyed researching and writing it. What a great excuse to go poking around in some of the scariest places known to man! This book is the first in a series about the *most haunted* hotels and inns, historic sites, and houses. If a place is not discussed that you feel should be listed, it may be haunted but not among the *most haunted* or it may be discussed in one of the other books in this series.

For more information on other books I've written, to check out my Ghost Town, or to download dozens of free ghost and travel reports, visit www.terrancezepke.com.

Also, be sure to take the fun quiz I've included at the end of the book to see if you're ready to chase these ghosts!

Terrance Zepke

Trans-Allegheny Lunatic Asylum

Trans-Allegheny Lunatic Asylum

FUN FACTS:

The structure is listed on the U.S. National Register of Historic Places and is a U.S. National Historic Landmark.

Staff lived on site with dorm rooms for nurses and apartments for doctors and their families.

People could get locked up in the asylum for dozens of reasons, most having nothing to do with being mentally ill. For instance, you could be locked up for: being an alcoholic or drug user; men could commit their wives if they were disobedient or tiresome; women could be committed for being promiscuous, going through menopause or if suffering from bad PMS; being bad tempered; mentally slow or stupid;

Disabled; behaving badly or being weird; or if a family just wanted rid of a troublesome relative.

The History

In the early 1800s, the Virginia General Assembly authorized a hospital to be built in Weston for the mentally ill. Construction on the facility began in 1858 but it wasn't completed for twenty-three years due to the Civil War and other issues. Also known as the War Between the States, the Civil War lasted from 1861-1865, but forever changed our nation.

When Virginia seceded, the governor demanded the return of all funds that had been provided to build the hospital. But he was too late. Under the command of Colonel Tyler, the 7th Ohio Infantry got to Weston first. At 5 a.m. on June 30, 1961, the troops seized nearly $27,000 in gold from the Weston Branch of the Exchange Bank of Virginia. The soldiers left $2,371.23 in the bank because that was the amount currently owed to creditors and for wages. The men took the money to Wheeling where it would be used to establish a new government. The soldiers were also supposed to apprehend anyone suspected of being a Confederate sympathizer, but their main objective was the loot.

West Virginia became a state on June 20, 1863. Throughout the war, the partially-constructed hospital became a military post known as Camp Tyler. The southern part of the hospital became barracks. Today, this is reportedly one of the most haunted parts of the building. Food and clothing that had been purchased for the first patients of the hospital were stolen by marauders. During the war, Union and Confederate troops took turns taking control of this military post.

Thanks to the hospital, this area was one of the few that did not suffer a post-war depression. To the contrary, it created a strong economy for the county. The first patients were finally admitted in the fall of 1864, but construction continued through 1881. Because of its remote location, the hospital had to be self-sufficient. At one time, the grounds extended 666 acres and included a dairy, waterworks, farm, and cemetery.

The 242,000-square-foot building is the largest hand-cut stone masonry building in North America and the second largest in the world after the Kremlin in Moscow, Russia. It was designed to maximize fresh air and sunshine. Prisoners accomplished the initial construction while skilled masons were imported from Ireland and Germany to hand-cut and lay the stone. The Gothic Revival and Tudor Revival style architecture is what makes the structure so imposing. Originally, it was supposed to accommodate 250 people, but by the 1950s, there were roughly 2,500 patients, making for poor conditions for patients and staff.

One of the former long-time nurses at the hospital is now a part-time tour guide. She shared some intriguing stories with me. The era when she was employed at the hospital was long before the current rules and regulations existed. She said there were often only two or three nurses for every 100-200 patients on a ward. She recalls being overpowered by a strong female patient who stole her keys and nearly escaped one night. She is sure the patient would have gotten away if another patient had not called for help on her behalf. She recalls one patient was murdered in his bed by another patient who got fed up with his snoring. She shivered when she spoke of the screams that could be heard during "treatments."

Dangerous experiments were performed on patients, such as electroshock therapy and lobotomies. Punishments for troublesome patients included cage-like cribs hung from the ceiling and cold water baths. Therapies included hydrotherapy, which was when patients were emerged in temperature-controlled water while laying on a hammock on top of a bathtub, covered with a canvas sheet with a hole cut out for their heads to stick out. Primitive-looking tools are on display in museum rooms on the first floor, along with craft projects made by patients as part of their therapy.

The hospital closed in May 1999 when a modern facility was built to replace the old hospital. Many attempts to do something with the property were made but failed. Some of these included a museum, hotel complex, and golf course. Finally, the building was auctioned off in 2007. A contractor from Morganton, West Virginia won the bid at $1.5 million. Joe Jordan took possession of the property in early 2008. His family, including his daughter, her husband, and his granddaughter, maintain the property and operate tours and special events.

The Hauntings

A child named Lilly is believed to haunt the place. At that time, if a parent was put in this kind of facility, the child was also placed here if there was no one else to take care of the child. It was an incredibly lonely and sad childhood for poor Lilly. Some time ago, an employee brought a doll and a red ball for Lilly. No matter where these items are left at closing time, they are always found elsewhere the next day. Visitors sometimes leave hard candy or a piece of gum in different places during the tour. Sometimes they have been moved or disappear before the tour even ends!

Of all the haunted places I've visited, this is the creepiest place I've ever investigated. You just have an overwhelming feeling of sadness while inside the building and a constant feeling of an unseen presence all around you. And when I say unseen presence I mean I felt there were lots of spirits lingering in that old building and I felt several were all around me at several points during my visit, especially on the fourth floor. I did experience cold sensations but that may not be ghostly. The building is not heated so there cold pockets throughout, especially on the fourth floor. In fact, it is usually colder inside the building than outside on any given winter's day.

It is believed that some of the tortured souls who were locked up here may still be here, as well as some of the men and women who died during experimental treatments and procedures. The spirit of the man who was murdered in his sleep and others who died as a result of illness and old age may also linger here.

Many ghost groups have investigated this place, including the renowned TAPS. In 2008, they declared it haunted. Ghost Adventures conducted an overnight investigation in 2009. They too declared it haunted having experienced lots of paranormal activity. One such event later led to great controversy. An EMF detector was flung out of an investigator's hand during the live taping. Viewers believe that the investigator, who is not part of the Ghost Adventures team, threw the device rather than it being jerked away from him by an unseen presence. The investigator maintains his story that it was seized by a supernatural entity.

Visitor Information

Trans-Allegheny Lunatic Asylum is open late March – October 31. There are several tour options, including a Civil War tour, photography tour, history tour, and short (first floor only) and long tours (all four floors). Special events are offered seasonally. We took a long tour during the day that is a must for seeing everything and learning all about its history. We also opted for the late night haunted flashlight tour that was eerie, but not nearly as much as the overnight paranormal lockdown we bravely signed up for. There were strange sounds throughout the night and a constant feeling of ghosts everywhere, but I did not see any ghosts or capture anything unusual on camera. The doll was moved from where I had placed it at some point in the evening. No one claimed to have moved it. However, the piece of candy I put out for Lilly was where I had left it.

There is a haunted house, fall festival, and Halloween Asylum Ball in October. There is discussion about adding more special events so be sure to check their website. Also, there are public and private ghost hunts. Groups must be insured or may purchase insurance policy through the asylum.

Visitor Information

71 Asylum Drive

Weston, WV 26452.

Weston is two hours from Pittsburgh, PA; 5 hours from Charlotte, NC; and 4 hours from Lexington, KY.

http://www.trans-alleghenylunaticasylum.com

Moon River Brewing Company

Moon River Brewing Company

FUN FACTS:

Moon River Brewing Company is in the heart of Savannah's Historic District. In addition to being haunted, it happens to serve good food and beer.

It used to be a hotel, bar, gambling hall, bank, and post office. Many important people stayed here when it was a hotel, including Revolutionary War hero Marquis de Lafayette, War of 1812 hero Winfield Scott, three U.S. Navy commodores, and naturalist James Audubon lived at the hotel for six months while he tried to sell his wildlife books.

The place is believed to be haunted by the spirit of a man who lost his life here during a duel. Dueling was a popular and legal means to settle disputes at one time. But it was much more than that. A duel was perceived as a way to gain satisfaction and restore honor. There were terms that had to be agreed upon by both parties, such as weapons (i.e. pistols or swords), and locations (i.e. in a field or down by the river) and time of day (i.e. dawn or high noon). Many famous men have been linked to duels, such as Andrew Jackson, Lord Wellington, Aaron Burr, Alexander Hamilton, and Abraham Lincoln.

The History

The Moon River Brewing Company was formerly the first hotel in Savannah. The City Hotel was built in 1821 by Elazer Early of Charleston. When it opened in 1826, the hotel also served as a bank, bar, and post office. Imagine being able to make a deposit, spend the night, eat a hot meal, mail a letter, and have a drink all in the same place.

In 1851, Peter Wiltberger bought the hotel. During the 1850s, he put two lions on exhibit in the lobby. What a marketing ploy! The beautiful creatures drew lots of attention and business—up until 1864 when it was forced to shut down. That's when General Sherman conducted his 'March to the Sea' military campaign. Sherman and his troops left Atlanta on November 16 and made their way to Savannah where he captured the port city on December 21.

After that, the building was used to store lumber and coal. Later, it was used for storage and office space. The roof was ripped off the building during Hurricane David in 1979. The building was vacant from 1979 until 1995 when renovations began to turn the old hotel into a microbrewery and restaurant. The Moon River Brewing Company opened on April 10, 1999. In addition to having a great selection of beer, it is known as the most haunted place in Savannah. Ever since that time, people have had ghostly encounters.

 The Hauntings

"Upstairs is where the ghost resides," Karen told us as she pointed to the old stairwell.

The staff graciously shared their stories and answered all my questions and took me all over the building, except to the top floor where no one is allowed because it is unsafe and where the ghost likes to hang out when not scaring folks in the bar. I spent one whole evening at Moon River Brewing Company enjoying good food and drink, as well as researching one of the most haunted places in the city.

Here's what I learned. It all began in 1832. James Jones Stark was drinking heavily in the hotel's bar. He was what was known as a rebel rouser. He was a heavy drinker and frequent gambler who often became a mean drunk and a sore loser, so he often ended up in brawls. One night he began making disparaging remarks about another patron, Dr. Phillip Minis, during a game of coins. When Minis won the game, Stark did not take it well. He accused Minis of cheating and began to yell and curse at him.

Stark challenged Minis to a duel. He chose rifles at paces at 5 p.m. at the river. Minis said the duel had to be pistols at paces at a different time and location. The duel never happened because they two men couldn't agree on terms. The next time they ran into each other, the men got into a fight. They threw a few punches, but it was quickly broken up. Stark continued to bad mouth Minis to anyone who would listen. Minis grew fearful that the bad talk was hurting his reputation.

On August 9, 1832 things came to a head. Minis confronted Stark at the City Hotel. He was angry and fed up with the things Stark had said about him. He sent someone upstairs to Stark's room to get him. When Stark came downstairs, Minis called him a "coward" and a "liar." Stark, furious at Minis for these comments, lunged for the man. Minis pulled out a gun and fatally shot Stark. Remarkably, Minis was acquitted at trial. The jury believed what he did was justified because he was in fear for his life. Although Stark did not have a weapon on him at that time, the logic of the jury was that he was a real threat to Minis. Furthermore, Minis had his reputation to protect. As Samuel Johnson said, *"A man may shoot the man who invades his character, as he may shoot him who attempts to break into his house."*

The logic was simple: a man's honor was everything, so his reputation had to be safeguarded at all costs. When this was called into question, a duel was often the best way to resolve the situation. Duels could be fought using different weapons, such as swords, pistols, rifles, or knives. Since duels were intended to restore honor, death was not necessary. Only twenty percent of duels ended in death. Andrew Jackson survived fourteen duels.

James Jones Stark has haunted the property ever since his murder. A shadowy figure has been seen that most believe is Stark, who remains unsatisfied with the outcome of that ill-fated night. The sounds of a game of pool being played are heard, but no one is ever found playing pool. The cue ball is sometimes seen moving across the table but no one has hit it and there is no breeze or logical reason for the movement.

A brewery employee was in the office one night doing paperwork when a bottle flew off the shelf and across the room. He heard footsteps on the stairwell but found no one there. Unnerved, he set the alarm and left. Another employee was sitting at the bar one night with some friends. They watched silverware move around on a table as if someone were rearranging it and then watched it drop to the floor, as if someone threw it down.

A few years ago, an antique desk appeared in an empty room on the second floor. No one knew how it got there. It disappeared three weeks later. No one claimed responsibility for the appearance or disappearance. Once, an employee was in the basement and was violently slapped four times by the ghost.

It is believed that there is another ghost at Moon River besides Stark. Employees have heard their names called by a woman but no one is there when they turn around to answer. An apparition in white is seen on occasion stumbling down the stairs. When it was the City Hotel, there were guest rooms upstairs. The clientele was diversified, ranging from respectable businessmen to the likes of James Jones Stark. She may have been a prostitute or jilted lover. The torso of a Union soldier was seen in 2007 by a police officer, but I didn't find any research or other people who have seen the torso ghost.

The ghosts do not like renovations. Whenever work is done on the old building, tools turn up missing, moved, or are thrown across a room. When work was being done in the late 1990s to turn the building into a brewery, a construction foreman's wife was pushed down the stairs by an invisible force when she brought lunch for her husband one afternoon.

How many ghosts linger here? Besides Stark and the woman in white, a little girl in a light-colored dress has been seen. It is believed to be the spirit of a child who died of yellow fever. For a while, the hotel was converted to a hospital during a yellow fever epidemic. The fourth floor housed the sick children. However, a little boy named Toby has been seen on occasion in the basement.

The most haunted areas are the basement and upstairs. Dragging sounds have been heard in the basement but no one is found whenever a brave soul goes to investigate. Knocking, footsteps, and chains rattling have also been heard. Were slaves or prisoners kept in the basement at one time? There are underground tunnels that have been found throughout Savannah, including the exterior of one at Moon River that appears to have been sealed up many years ago.

During a book party at the restaurant, one of the guests went with a group down into the basement. She did not believe in ghosts and said as much to someone who was sharing a ghost story. The publisher was choked, pushed, and grabbed by her neck by an invisible force.

Which ghost attacked this woman? Which ghost might you encounter during a visit to Moon River Brewing Company? Check out their website to see haunted footage that employees and visitors have captured on film and video.

Visitor Information

Moon River is open year round.

21 W. Bay Street.

Savannah, Georgia 31401.

www.moonriverbrewingcompany.com

It is 3 hours and fifty-five minutes from Atlanta, Georgia to Savannah. It is 12 hours and 814 miles from New York City. The distance is 468 miles, which takes roughly seven hours to get from Richmond, Virginia to Savannah.

Terrance Zepke

Eastern State
Penitentiary

Eastern State Penitentiary

FUN FACTS:

Penitentiary means correctional facility, detention camp, detention center, house of correction, house of detention, jail, lockup, penal colony, penal institution, penal settlement, place of confinement, place of detention, place of imprisonment, reformatory, and/or prison. ESP was the first penitentiary in the world.

Prisoners had to become like monks who took vows of silence. They were not allowed to talk and were subjected to horrific punishment if caught doing so. ESP was home to more than 80,000 male and female inmates.

A dog became the first and only non-human inmate when Pennsylvania Governor Pinchot sentenced Pep to a life sentence for killing Mrs. Pinchot's cat. He was assigned an inmate number: C2559. However, many dismiss this report believing that the governor donated the dog to the prison. It was believed that taking care of pets and tending a prison garden helped with prisoner morale.

The History

Eastern State Penitentiary was originally called Cherry Hill and was the first penitentiary the world. The grand Gothic-style design was also the most expensive and remains one of the most famous. The project was approved in 1821 and the prison opened on October 25, 1829, but construction was not complete until 1836. The facility with its radial or "hub and spoke" plan became the model for more than 300 prisons worldwide. Built to accommodate 450 prisoners, the facility was designed and built by John Haviland. Haviland is a renowned architect who used the best asylums, prisons, and churches of Europe, that were built circa 1780s, as his basis.

The result is a daunting structure that strikes fear into inmates and is meant to discourage would-be criminals. Haviland is considered the most influential prison architect to this day. The radial plan he conceived meant that there were seven cell wings that were built in semi-circles with an octagonal tower being the central point. This guaranteed 24/7 surveillance. The rotunda is in the exact center of the prison. Thirty-foot walls discouraged escape attempts.

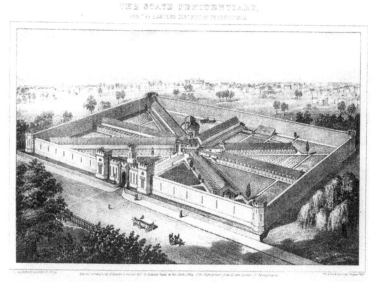

The first three cellblocks were one-story and housed forty good-sized cells. The heated cells were 8 x 12 x 10. Each had a water tap (even the White House did not have running water at this time), flush toilet, a bunk bed that was chained to the wall, and personal exercise yard enclosed with a ten-foot wall. The concrete cells had short metal doors that were covered with thick wooden doors to control noise. One popular theory is that the doors were sized this way so that prisoners had to "bow" to enter or exit, thus reminding them of their penance. There was a small glass skylight in each cell that has been dubbed the "Eye of God" because prisoners could look up to heaven and reflect that God is always with them. Again, the concept of penance is prevalent. The other four cellblocks were two-story cells. In keeping with their penance and no talking policies, prisoners were hooded whenever they were removed from their cells. This wasn't often given that prisoners were required to be in their cells most of the time.

Cell Block #15, also known as "Death Row," was reserved for the worst criminals. They were considered violent and extremely dangerous. They had no interaction with other prisoners, including having their own exercise yard. The concept is known as the Pennsylvania System, which was an experiment in solitary confinement and reform.

The most famous prisoners were Al Capone, "Slick Willie" Sutton, Morris "The Rabbi" Bolber, William "Blackie" Zupkoski, and Freda Frost. She was the last female inmate at the prison. She received a twenty-year sentence for murdering her spouse. She successfully poisoned her "no good husband." Capone served almost one year at ESP. During that time, he was allowed to furnish his cell with rugs, antique furniture, and oil paintings! According to legend, he broke up a fight and that led to the warden being grateful enough to let him decorate his cell. But most think it is more likely that Capone bribed officials.

The biggest prison escape occurred on April 3, 1945. "Slick Willie" Sutton and eleven other inmates dug a tunnel to freedom. They spent the better part of a year digging this tunnel, which extended under the prison wall. Despite their best efforts, they were caught. Unbelievably, thirty more tunnels were found during renovations in the 1930s.

Given that there was so much emphasis on forgiveness and reform, it is interesting that such harsh punishments were distributed to disobedient prisoners. The inmates were not allowed to communicate, the idea being that silence was part of the penance process. This was a time to reflect on and atone for their sins. If they were caught talking or breaking other rules, they were subjected to a "cold water bath," "mad chair," and "iron gag."

The cold water bath involved taking prisoners outside into the cold winter weather and then dousing them with ice cold water. The mad chair was when prisoners were strapped into chairs for long periods of time. The iron gag was the worst. A steel gag was used to secure the tongue and the other end was tied to the wrists. If they did not remain perfectly still, the tie cut into the tongue causing significant pain and bodily damage. Given these awful torture treatments, perhaps "The Hole" wasn't so bad! This is when prisoners were thrown into solitary confinement. The cell was dark as a hole and the prisoners sat or lay on the floor or stood in the dark confinement for hours or days on end.

Prisoners were permitted to exercise, tend a garden, and take care of prison pets. The silent system was abandoned in 1913. From that time on, prisoners were allowed to speak to one another and to receive visitors.

The facility was closed permanently in 1971. It sat abandoned for more than twenty years. During that time, it was nearly developed into a mall, apartment complex and other commercial projects. Thankfully, the prison was saved and has been a National Historic Landmark since 1966. It opened for public tours in 1994. A good resource for more information is the publication, *Eastern State Penitentiary: A History* (History Press, 2008). It was written by a former tour guide with the help of other ESP employees.

The Hauntings

The most haunted areas of the prison seem to be Cellblock #4 and Cellblock #12. The most common report is strange sounds, such as footsteps and cries when no one is there. Some visitors have complained of out-of-body experiences. Amateur ghost hunters often claim to capture ghostly images and orbs on their cameras. TAPS has footage from an investigation that shows what appears to be a specter.

The camera captured what appears to be a shadowy figure disappearing down the corridor of Cellblock 12. Several members of the crew also had encounters. Two team members saw a black mass or small shadow in a couple of different places along the hallway but quickly lost sight of it. When a similar encounter took place with two other team members who were taking photographs, they got so spooked that they ran out of the building! TAPS went back to debunk what they saw (and I suspect salvage their reputation after having two team members flee the building like scared little girls) but were unable to disprove paranormal activity. They knew it was either a manifestation or a hoax, but after two more nights at ESP, they could not disprove a paranormal encounter, despite bringing in special equipment and additional crew members.

To the contrary, the investigators are convinced that ESP is haunted. It is included among their list of most haunted places. They had many reasons for their conclusion after several visits: seeing what was presumably a spectral, difficulty breathing, hair standing up on the back of their necks, feelings of dread and anxiety, whispers and footsteps, heaviness, and a feeling of being watched (especially on the third floor of cellblock).

It's not just visitors who have experienced supernatural encounters. Inmates as far back as the 1940s reported paranormal activity. Footage from various ghost investigations conducted over the years can be seen on ESP's site, www.easternstate.org/ghosts.

Visitor Information

2027 Fairmount Avenue

Philadelphia, PA 19130

www.easternstate.org

There is a visitor's center on site and the place is open every day (except holidays) for tours, including winter adventure tours. "Terror Behind the Walls" is a nightly haunted attraction created in 1991 by the Eastern State Penitentiary Historic Site Inc., which operates the museum (also known as a "preserved ruin"). It includes several attractions, including a 3-D haunted house. It is one of the first of such attractions in America.

Philadelphia is 2 hours and fifty minutes from Washington, DC (136 miles); 7 hours or 430 miles from Raleigh, North Carolina; and 999 miles (16 hours) from Orlando, Florida.

Terrance Zepke

Shanghai Tunnels

Shanghai Tunnels

FUN FACTS:

Portland has many nicknames, such as "Shanghai Capital of the World," "Worst Port in the World," "City of Roses," "Forbidden City," and "Unheavenly City." Most are related to its history of shanghaiing.

Men could go out for a few drinks and wake up at sea if they drank at the wrong place! Women were also abducted and forced into prostitution.

The tunnels are open to the public and visitors can choose from a variety of tour options, such as the "Shanghai Tunnel Ethnic History Tour" and "Shanghai Tunnel Ghost Tour."

The History

Merchants dug a network of tunnels under the city to transport merchandise to the water because it was easier than using the muddy, crowded streets to get the items to waiting ships. The tunnels also became a perfect way to handle human trafficking or shanghaiing.

Shanghaiing was an illegal activity but one that was widespread. It happened in Oregon and all over the world. Part of the problem is that local authorities and law enforcement denied its existence, tending to pretend it was not a problem.

By the mid-1800s, maritime trade was booming and there were not enough men for the crews, especially due to the Gold Rush. Ships from all over came to town and spent money while "shopping" for sailors. Also, it cut down on the transient and undesirable population. And shanghaiing served to fill a real need so perhaps they thought they were doing their civic duty!

Captains were always short-handed and resorted to some disturbing practices to find able-bodied men. They hired men, known as "shanghaiiers" to help them get good men. This was accomplished going to waterfront taverns where there was lots of drinking and commotion. During the course of the night, men were plied with drinks and a good meal that might be doped with a sleep aid. When the men fell asleep or passed out, they were taken to holding cells.

Once the shanghaiiers were paid the fees, they turned the men over to the captains. They were then transported to waiting ships through a series of tunnels that extended across a city (and under key buildings and businesses) down to the waterfront.

For approximately one hundred years, shanghaiing happened in waterfront towns all over the world. Among the places with the highest incidents was Portland, Oregon. It is believed that more than 2,000 people were shanghaied here during 1850 – 1940. Some put the figure much higher. Regardless of the exact number, it is obvious why Portland has been nicknamed "The Shanghai Capital of the World."

Sailors, loggers, farmers, gypsies, ranchers,

cowboys, pirates, transients, and any other healthy male who frequented establishments with tunnel access underneath, such as Snug Harbor Saloon, Valhalla Saloon, Lazlo's Saloon, and Erickson's Saloon were likely to wake up somewhere far away. Reportedly, it took two full voyages or six years, for these men to get back home to Portland. Most of the ships were headed far away—to Shanghai, China. This is how the practice came to be called "shanghaiing."

A remarkably sophisticated system of tunnels snaked their way across the city from the North End (Old Town and Chinatown) to the South End (downtown). The tunnels, known now as the Portland Underground, were built under places that were likely to draw men, such as saloons, brothels, gambling parlors, and opium dens. Transients, such as cowboys, sheep herders, and migrant farmers were ideal victims. After they had been plied with so much alcohol as to be drunk enough not to put up a fight (or given knock out drops), they were lured away to well-placed trap doors.

Men waited in the tunnel under the trap door for the men and women to be dropped. They caught the drunk or drugged bodies and dragged them to holding cells to await their fate. Their shoes were taken to impede escape and broken glass was reportedly scattered through the tunnels in case they came to and managed to escape their holding cells. Just before a ship's departure, the victim was again given knock out drops and carried to the waiting vessel. By the time the victim woke up, he would be far away.

During archaeological digs, old shoes have been found in the tunnels, substantiating the stories about the removed shoes.

 The Hauntings

It's no wonder these 6' x 6' holding cells and tunnels are haunted what with so much misery and tragedy. And it wasn't just men. Women were often abducted and forced into prostitution. If they refused, they were murdered. Men and women were drugged and carried out secret basement doors to the holding cells and tunnels. However, some never made it any farther. Some died as a result of the fall of being thrown or dropped through the secret trap doors.

One spirit that haunts these tunnels is believed to a woman who died when deposited into a holding cell. Today, the business is a pizzeria but back when it was a shanghai hotspot; Nina was hustling business one night when she was drugged and thrown down into the holding cell. She hit her head and suffered internal injuries that resulted in her death. Ever since that time, her spirit haunts this place. She has been seen, her perfume smelled, and she has been known to tug on the clothing of tour participants.

But Nina is not the only ghost in these tunnels. There are believed to be several spirits unhappily trapped here. Their presence is shown in many ways, such as faint whispers, moans, cries, strange lights and shapes that appear in photos, and the smell of alcohol and cologne.

Tour operators installed thirteen sets of wind chimes in the tunnels. They call them "spirit chimes." Whenever they swing or ring, that means the spirits are nearby because there is no air flow to trigger the chimes.

There were a few prostitution rooms in the tunnel. A sheet hung like a curtain covered a small bed. There were rooms above the saloon that were also used for prostitution, but those were 'willing participants'. The shanghaied women were kept in the tunnels or sold into slavery.

Ghost groups have detected paranormal activity using EVPs, thermal imaging, and shadow detectors, which show unexplainable light shadowy mist. Some visitors to the tunnels report feeling lightheaded, dizzy and/or queasy feeling. Unexplained footsteps are heard and the sounds of old doors "creaking" open.

Visitor Information

Tours are offered by the non-profit group, Cascade Geographic Society. They last ninety minutes and explain the history and haunting of these tunnels. Special seasonal ghost tours are offered during October.

http://www.portlandtunnels.com/index.html

Portland is 3 hours (173 miles) from Seattle, Washington and 15 hours (962 miles) from Los Angeles, California.

Waverly Hills Sanatorium

Waverly Hills Sanatorium

FUN FACTS:

This place was built to treat tuberculosis patients, but often times the disease was fatal. It was considered bad for morale for all the corpses to be seen by patients. Since the hospital was built on a hill, a rail and cable system was devised for transporting the bodies from a "body chute" to the bottom of the hill where a train was waiting to carry the deceased away. This was a secret system, unknown to the patients at Waverly.

In earlier times, tuberculosis was known as consumption. As the highly infectious disease spread, it was nicknamed "white death" and "white plague." People who had TB were called "lungers."

During the 17th and 18th centuries, twenty-five percent of all deaths in Europe were attributed to TB. Early treatments of the disease included drinking garlic and dog fat potions, breathing smoke from burning cow dung, placing seaweed under a patient's bed, and taking long sea voyages to encourage vomiting, which exercised the chest. Since the lowest number of TB cases occurred in people living near the ocean, it was believed that living at the water helped with recovery.

The History

The property was once owned by Thomas H. Hayes. He bought it because he had to build a school for his daughters to attend since there was not one nearby. He constructed a one-room schoolhouse and hired a teacher named Lizzie Lee Harris. Harris is the one who came up with Waverly School, which Hayes liked so much that he called his property, Waverly Hill. He later sold the land and a hospital was built on his former property. The Board of Tuberculosis Hospital also liked the name a lot. So much so that they called their new facility The Waverly Hills Sanatorium.

Originally, the structure was a simple two-story wood building with two open-air pavilions. It was meant to accommodate 40-50 tuberculosis patients. This hospital opened on July 26, 1910. Tuberculosis was a highly contagious, deadly disease. TB patients had to be quarantined. It was believed that recovery was dependent on lots of fresh air, a soothing environment, and ample rest.

Sadly, tuberculosis, also known as the "white plague" or "white death," quickly became an epidemic. Entire families and small towns were wiped out. The hospital was soon overflowing with patients—three times as many as was intended. People infected with TB were sometimes referred to as "lungers."

Nowadays, there are drugs that a patient can take to treat it, but at that time, there were no antibiotics to combat this serious illness. One in every seven deaths in Europe in the late 1800s was from TB. It spread quickly during the age of the industrial revolution. The small facility was not sufficient to house and treat the growing number of TB patients.

A five-story hospital was approved and construction began in March 1924. Six months later, the impressive facility opened its doors. It was built to house 400-500 patients and the imposing hospital with its Gothic Revival style design was considered the best sanatorium in America. By the early 1930s, there were approximately 700 TB hospitals in the United States. The powerful antibiotic streptomycin was discovered in the early 1940s. This was the beginning of the end of TB although there are still outbreaks in some parts of the world.

Although there was no cure for TB, it seemed that fresh air, healthy eating, and lots of bed rest could often restore a person's health. The fresh air was considered so important that patients were left outside for hours in comfortable chairs—even in the middle of winter with snow falling!

The Waverly Hills Sanatorium had a high success rate. Even so, their experimental treatments left much to be desired. Patients' lungs were exposed to ultra-violet light in the hopes of stopping the spread of the deadly bacteria. Balloons were inserted into the lungs and then filled with air with the idea that it would expand the lungs and improve breathing. Sometimes, ribs were removed to allow lung expansion and increase the flow of oxygen. Not surprisingly, these procedures usually resulted in death so they were reserved for patients who were in the worst condition and had nothing to lose.

Thankfully, TB was all but eradicated in most of the world by 1943. The facility was no longer needed and closed down in 1961. It reopened one year later as a nursing home, Woodhaven Geriatrics Sanitarium. Patients were reportedly mistreated and subjected to poor conditions. The state closed the facility in 1982.

By 2001, the place had been abandoned for nearly twenty years and was in terrible shape. Vagrants, vandals, and partying teenagers had also wreaked havoc on the deteriorating building. Remarkably, Charlie and Tina Mattingly saw something worth saving. They bought the place and began working with the local historical society to properly restore the property.

The Hauntings

Reportedly, there is a man wearing a white coat that may be the spirit of a former doctor. The figure is usually seen walking through the old kitchen. The smell of food cooking on the stove or bread baking in the oven can be smelled in the kitchen area even though it hasn't been used in many years. The fifth floor is supposed to be one of the most haunted areas of the building. When the place was operational, it held a pantry, linen closet, medicine room, and two nurses' stations with a room attached to each. Voices have been heard and ghostly sightings have occurred. Why is this area so haunted? One popular theory is that the TB patients who suffered mental breakdowns were housed in the rooms off the nurses' stations.

The hospital soon gained a reputation for being haunted and stories began to circulate of resident ghosts like the little girl who was seen running up and down the third floor solarium, the little boy who was spotted with a leather ball, the hearse that appeared in the back of the building dropping off coffins, the woman with the bleeding wrists who cried for help and others. Visitors told of slamming doors, lights in the windows as if power was still running through the building, strange sounds and eerie footsteps in empty rooms.

Visitor Information

Guided tours and paranormal investigations are offered throughout the year. An annual haunted house attraction is offered seasonally and a laser light show is shown during the Christmas season.

4400 Paralee Lane

Louisville, KY 40272

www.therealwaverlyhills.com

It is 2 hours and forty-five minutes (174 miles) from Nashville, Tennessee to Louisville. The distance is 259 miles (4 hours) from St. Louis, Missouri to Louisville.

Terrance Zepke

Pirates' House

Pirates' House

FUN FACTS:

The illegal activity known as shanghaiing was done here. Remnants of the shanghai tunnels can still be seen today.

The most haunted rooms are the Captain's Room and the Herb House.

Popular stories about Captain Flint haunting this place are most likely untrue. However, men were shanghaied into service by desperate captains. It was pre-arranged that an 'agent' was paid a fee to help a sea captain or pirate captain capture unwitting men.

A hardy-looking young man who was "three sheets to the wind" was the best target. They were lured outside or downstairs where they could be transported to the waiting ship. Many years ago, a police officer claimed he had been drugged and forced into three years of service. He was carried down to the rum cellar and through the tunnel. In 1948, a tunnel was discovered during renovation and filled in, but the remains can still be seen in a corner of the restaurant.

The History

Originally, this restaurant was a house. Later, it became a tavern and much later, a restaurant. Some say it was built in 1753, while others claim it was around 1794. Over time, lots of additions were made to the building. When it became a restaurant, these add-ons became twelve dining rooms.

The main level was a restaurant/bar and the upstairs had rooms for rent when the property was an inn for seamen. Sailors on leave rented rooms upstairs, which was convenient after a late night of drinking.

There is a basement, which is where the tunnel is located. It runs from the house down to the river. Some say that men, who got too drunk in the tavern, awoke to find themselves on pirate ships, transported to the ship through the tunnel. When these tunnels were built remains unknown. It may relate to slavery or piracy. The remains of a tunnel can be seen today by patrons of The Pirates' House.

 The Hauntings

Maybe that is why the spirit of a sailor has been seen on the first floor of The Pirates' House and what appears to be a pirate captain who died in one of the upstairs rooms roams the upstairs and the basement. The shadowy figure is big and rough-looking and is dressed like a pirate captain. Over the years, this spirit has been seen late at night on occasion by a manager as he or she crosses the room to exit after completing closing duties. The startled manager, who thought that he or she was alone, usually turns around to say something to the man—but the figure has disappeared as quickly as it appeared.

Employees have heard cursing and laughing upstairs, but no one is ever found when someone investigates the noises. A voice calling out *"Get me more rum!"* has been heard. Dining room chairs are rearranged almost every night and doors open for no reason. Screams have been heard coming from the basement when no one is down there. In 2009, major renovations were made to the property, including the removal of roughly thirty-five percent of The Hideaways (tunnel system).

The Paranormal Ghost Hunters of North Georgia have conducted two investigations. The first was inconclusive but the second investigation revealed ghostly voices recorded on the EVP.

When visiting, be sure to ask to be seated in the Captain's Room, which is the most haunted area of the building, along with the Herb House. The Captain's Room is where these seamen once partied, fought, and were shanghaied into servitude. It is believed that the spirits of some of these men still haunt the place.

One of the waiters shared a personal experience

with us. He explained that one day he came into the Captain's Room at the start of his shift to check his station. Soon afterwards, table candles blew out and the door began swinging wildly like someone had just come charging through it. He said he suddenly felt a little nauseas and apprehensive.

Visitor Information

The restaurant is on the outskirts of Savannah's Historic District.

20 East Broad Street

Savannah, GA 31401

www.thepirateshouse.com

It takes 2.5 hours (159 miles) to get from Columbia, South Carolina to Savannah. It is 665 miles (10.5 hours) to reach Savannah from Louisville, Kentucky.

Terrance Zepke

Bobby Mackey's Music World

Bobby Mackey's Music World

FUN FACTS:

This bar has been a slaughterhouse, cult clubhouse, nightclub, speakeasy, casino, and a Hard Rock Café.

It has probably been featured on more shows than any other haunted place in America.

Bobby Mackey knew the minute he saw the building that he had to own it and operate a nightclub on the premises, even though he had no experience and never had any intention of owning a bar.

The History

This honky-tonk was originally a slaughterhouse, dating back to the 1850s. It was one of the biggest packing houses in the area until it closed down in the 1890s.

Devil worshippers used the basement of the vacant building for satanic rituals, which included animal sacrifices. These horrific practices were accidentally discovered in 1896 during the murder investigation of Pearl Bryan.

Pearl was the youngest of twelve children. She was also the most attractive with bright blue eyes, soft blond hair, and a peaches-and-cream complexion. Her natural good looks brought many suitors, including a young man named Scott Jackson. They met when Pearl's cousin, William Woods, introduced her to his new friend, a fellow student at Ohio College. The twenty-two-year-old beauty was smitten with the young man from their first meeting. Jackson was studying dentistry. Pearl's family was overjoyed when the pair began dating since Jackson was from a prominent family from Maine and he was pursuing a good career.

They surely wouldn't have been so pleased if they knew the whole story. The twenty-eight-year-old dental student was also a member of the occult group that met in the basement of the old slaughterhouse. Not only was he a devil worshipper, he had an intimate relationship with Pearl. She ended up pregnant, but Jackson was not ready to get married and become a father. With the help of her cousin, William Woods, Jackson talked Pearl into having an abortion, even though she was already almost five months pregnant.

The last time Pearl Bryan was ever seen by friends and family was on February 2, 1896. She told her parents that she was going to Indianapolis with Will. According to the plan that the threesome concocted, Pearl told her parents that her cousin was going home to visit friends and had invited her to come along, which was probably why they allowed her to go. Otherwise, it is highly unlikely that they would have let her travel alone.

But Will didn't accompany Pearl and she didn't go to Indianapolis. Instead, she went to Cincinnati to meet her boyfriend and his roommate, Alonzo Walling. Walling was also a dental student at the college. It's unclear whether Pearl knew that Jackson planned to perform the procedure with Walling's help or if she believed she was going to a "clinic." Whatever the case, she went along with the plan.

Despite his assurances to Will, Jackson had no idea what he was doing. He tried to end the pregnancy using cocaine and dental tools and this resulted in great pain and bleeding. Presumably, Jackson and Walling panicked over the botched abortion. They didn't know what to do with the injured girl. Frightened and desperate, the young men concocted a hasty plan.

They took Pearl to a secluded area near Fort Thomas and committed a barbaric murder. They used dental tools to behead their victim. During the trial, a doctor testified that evidence showed that Pearl was alive when she was decapitated. Pearl's body was found a mile and a half away from the former slaughterhouse where Jackson and his group performed animal sacrifices while worshipping Satan. Pearl Bryan's head was never found.

The two young men were soon charged with poor Pearl's murder and brought to trial in 1897. Walling testified that the murder was all Jackson's idea. Woods was charged as an accomplice but charges were dropped in exchange for his testimony against Walling and Jackson. In his first interview with the police, Walling said that Jackson had toyed with the idea of poisoning Pearl rather than going through with the abortion. After the failed abortion, Jackson quickly changed gears and came up with the murder plan.

Walling and Jackson were found guilty and sentenced to death. They were promised life sentences in lieu of execution if they revealed where the head was hidden. The men refused to divulge this information that could have saved their lives. Why?

Reportedly, they were more afraid of betraying their cult than being executed. According to legend, the head was taken back to the slaughterhouse and used for satanic rituals.

Scott Jackson's trial lasted for nearly a month (April 21 – May 14). Alonzo Walling's trial also lasted for near one month (May 20 – June 18). Both were found guilty. They were hanged on March 21, 1897 in what turned out to be the last public hanging in Campbell County. Just before his execution, Walling swore that he would come back from the grave and haunt the area. Many believe he is one of the ghosts that linger here.

Pearl's headless body was buried at Forest Hill

Cemetery in Greencastle, Indiana.

The building sat empty until the 1920s when it became a speakeasy. During that time, several mob hits took place but the bodies were removed so that they would not be discovered. The mob did not want to draw attention to the place where illegal actions, such as drinking and gambling, took occurred. The speakeasy was no longer necessary once Prohibition ended in 1933.

Buck Brady bought the place and turned it into a legal drinking establishment and casino called Primrose, but the mob wasn't happy with the competition. They forced Buck to sell Primrose by vandalizing the property and scaring off customers. One gangster, Albert "Red" Masterson tried to murder Buck and Buck retaliated by trying to kill him. Buck finally reluctantly sold the place to the mob after putting a curse on it. He swore that no business would ever succeed here. Buck Brady killed himself in 1965. No one knows seems to know why. I wonder if he was killed by the mob and it made to look like a suicide.

The mob renamed the place "Latin Quarter." The new owners were arrested several times for illegal gambling. By 1955, authorities had confiscated all the gambling tables and slot machines.

In another dark chapter in this property's history, the owner's daughter, Johanna, became pregnant by one of the club's singers. When her father found out, the mobster had the singer killed. When Johanna found out what her father had done, she tried to kill him. When her poisoning attempt was unsuccessful, the distraught daughter killed herself. Her body was discovered in the basement. An autopsy revealed that she was five months into her pregnancy—just like Pearl Bryan.

By the 1970s, the establishment had been bought by the Hard Rock Café franchise. Within a few years, it was shut down by local authorities after multiple fatalities on the premises.

In 1978, Bobby and Janet Mackey bought the abandoned building. Bobby claims he never wanted to be a nightclub owner until he saw the place. As soon as he laid eyes on the building, he knew that was what he going to do. And as soon as Bobby Mackey's Music World opened its doors, it became a success.

The Hauntings

The place is reportedly haunted by the ghost of Johanna and perhaps Buck and Pearl and other unknown ghosts, including men who were murdered on site by the mob.

The first employee hired by the Bob Mackey was the caretaker. Carl Lawson lived in an apartment above the bar. He often worked after hours, repeatedly finding the lights turned on, doors unlocked, and the jukebox playing. Yet he was sure that he had locked up, turned off the lights, and unplugged the jukebox during the closing ritual. He swore he saw ghosts too, including Johanna, in the bar and in the basement. Lawson told folks all the weird things he had witnessed, but most people did not believe him. Only a few who knew the dark history of the place did. They told Lawson that the basement is known as "Hell's Gate."

Over time, other employees and patrons had their own strange encounters. Janet Mackey has seen ghosts on occasion and has smelled rose cologne, which was said to be what Johanna wore. Janet also had a terrifying experience. Once, she was picked up by an unseen presence and pushed down the basement stairs. She was five months pregnant at that time—just like Pearl and Johanna!

A customer sued the owners after he swore he was attacked in the men's restroom by an evil spirit. The case was eventually dismissed for lack of proof. An "enter at your own risk" kind of sign has been hung warning patrons that the place is haunted and that management is not responsible for any harm that may come to them. Things got so bad that an exorcism was performed in 1994, but it failed to get rid of the spirits that haunt Bobby Mackey's Music World. With such a grim history, is it any wonder that strange things happen here?

This building has probably been featured on more television shows than any haunted place in America, including Ghost Hunters, Ghost Adventures, A Haunting, Is It Real?, Geraldo, and Jerry Springer Show, as well as the subject of numerous documentaries and on the Internet, such as an interactive broadcast on www.livescifi.tv and an Internet series, *Return to Bobby Mackey's.* These investigations and specials yielded mixed results, ranging from zero paranormal findings to ghostly sightings and encounters.

Visitor Information

The bar is ten minutes from downtown Cincinnati and open to the public. Haunted tours are offered on Friday and Saturday nights for adults only, which include the catacombs under the nightclub. Also, there are weekday tours for all ages and private investigations are permitted for a fee. The information is on their website. There is an interesting book written about the haunting of Bobby Mackey's Music World titled *Hell's Gate* by Douglas Hensley. During the course of his research, he interviewed twenty-nine witnesses to paranormal activities, including police and clergymen.

44 Licking Pike

Wilder, KY 41071

www.bobbymackey.com

It is 5.5 hours (302 miles) from Pittsburgh, Pennsylvania to Wilder and 4 hours (252 miles) from Knoxville, Tennessee to Wilder.

Terrance Zepke

Colonial Park Cemetery

Colonial Park Cemetery

FUN FACTS:

Archaeologists have discovered nearly 8,700 unmarked graves, in addition to the more than 550 marked graves.

Some famous people buried in Colonial Park Cemetery include James Habersham (Acting Royal Governor of the Province 1771-1773); Archibald Bulloch (first President of Georgia); Samuel Elbert (Revolutionary War soldier and Governor of Georgia); and Lachlan McIntosh (Major General of the Continental Army). Major General Nathanael Greene was buried here until the grave was reinterred in Johnson Square in 1901. The impressive arch entrance was added in 1913 by the Savannah chapter of the Daughters of the American Revolution.

The cemetery closed in 1853 because of overcrowding. The city established Laurel Grove Cemetery and Cathedral Cemetery.

The History

The cemetery was established in 1750. At that time, it was the first and only cemetery in Savannah. Over the years, it was expanded several times to include more than six acres. After an expansion in 1789, the cemetery was opened for burial for persons of all denominations. Dueling was a popular way to settle disputes; so many dueling victims are buried here. Some headstones reveal interesting information, such as "He fell in a duel on the 16th of January, 1815, by the hand of a man who, a short time ago, would have been friendless but for him…" (James Wilde's headstone).

When a Yellow Fever Epidemic swept through Savannah in 1820, it claimed more than 700 lives. The cemetery closed in 1853 due to overcrowding and neglect. Laurel Grove and Bonaventure Cemeteries were erected. Some families had become so distraught over the poor conditions at Colonial Park that they moved loved ones to one of these newer cemeteries. Years ago, many of the gravestones were removed.

One source says that city officials felt that there were too many gravestones given that thousands have been buried here over the years. Their logic was that the markers were haphazardly placed all over, making it hard to get around the grounds now that the old cemetery had been converted into a public park.

The result is hundreds or possibly thousands of unmarked graves, which means that visitors are literally walking on top of corpses. A yellow fever epidemic wiped out ten percent of the city's population in 1820. Due to the many deaths in such a short period of time, hundreds were buried in mass graves. With mass graves and many graves missing tombstones, visitors are walking over the dead every time they come to Colonial Park.

It was the city's only cemetery from 1750 –

1853. At that time, no more burials were permitted in the overcrowded cemetery. During the Civil War, Union soldiers seized Savannah. They camped in the cemetery during the winter of 1864. They callously vandalized gravestones and robbed mausoleums and tombs—after removing the dead! According to some reports, soldiers removed bodies from numerous crypts so that they could use them as refuge from the cold. Most likely, these bodies were buried in a mass grave rather than returned to their original crypts—if these reports are true.

The city nearly tore down the cemetery but a lawsuit by Christ Church stopped that from happening. The court forced the city to protect and convert the old cemetery into a park. By the late 1800s, benches and paths had been added throughout the grounds. This was a good start, but hardly enough to placate the poor souls who had been disturbed from their final resting spot or who had been buried in a mass, unmarked grave.

Much later, markers were made by the Georgia Historical Commission and placed beside graves denoting important individuals or events, such as Button Gwinnet, who was a signer of the Declaration of Independence.

The Hauntings

Who are some of the ghosts of Colonial Park Cemetery?

We'll never know for sure, but it is believed that one ghost is Renee Rondolia Asch (or Rene Asche Rondolier, according to some sources). Renee had a lot of strikes against him: he was an orphan, he was disfigured, and he had mental health issues. It was said that he killed animals just to watch them die. And he liked to hang out in the cemetery. So, when two young girls were found dead in the cemetery, townsfolk became convinced that Renee killed them. He was lynched in the swamps not far from the cemetery. More murder victims were later found in the cemetery. But no one believed that they had convicted the wrong man. Folks felt sure that it was the spirit of Renee Rondolia Asch, exacting his revenge. Some even call the cemetery "Renee's Playground."

There was a woman who worked as a maid at the City Hotel. One night, she saw a guest leaving the hotel. She happened to be going in the same direction, so she followed the man down the street. Later, she swore that she saw him literally disappear at the gates of Colonial Park Cemetery.

Footage of a child running through the cemetery has been captured by a visitor. The boy seems to float up into a tree and then out of it and then vanishes. I've seen this film and I just can't say for sure what it is. It may be ghost or there may be another explanation.

Visitor Information

Colonial Park Cemetery became a city park in 1896. It is open to the public. The cemetery is on the southeast corner of Abercorn Street and Oglethorpe Avenue.

201 E. Oglethorpe Avenue.

http://www.visit-historic-savannah.com/colonial-park-cemetery.html

Savannah is 366 miles (6 hours) from Chattanooga, Tennessee and 255 miles (4 hours) from Charlotte, North Carolina.

Terrance Zepke

Lincoln Theatre

Lincoln Theatre

FUN FACTS:

This building is believed to be haunted by several ghosts, including the spirit of a stagehand named "Red."

This edifice has survived at least two major fires that destroyed many of the surrounding businesses and has been struck by lightning.

Some of the biggest names in showbiz have performed here, including Al Jolson, Bob Hope, Houdini, and Boris Karloff.

The History

The Priest Hotel opened in 1860 and was operated by Franklin Priest. It was later owned by Riley Deming and became the New Deming in 1880. It was sold to Augustine Wait in 1892, who renamed it the Arcade Hotel.

The hotel was remodeled a few years later and renamed The Decatur & Arcade Hotel. The property burned down in 1904 but was soon rebuilt. It caught fire again on April 21, 1915. This fire destroyed the building and several nearby buildings. Two hotel guests, William Graham and C.S. Guild, were killed in the fire. Other guests were reported missing but presumed to have escaped since no other bodies were found.

The fire started because some oily rags were left too close to the boiler. The oily rags resulted in a quick and fierce blaze. The surrounding buildings: YMCA, Presbyterian Church, Odd Fellows, and Bachman Bros. & Martin Co. were victims of the quick-spreading fire. The hotel was not rebuilt.

A theatre was built on the site in 1916. The idea was conceived by Clarence Wait, who inherited the land and envisioned it as the perfect place for a downtown theatre. He hired the architectural firm of Aschauer & Waggoner. They did a fine job creating one of the best theatres in America. The lovely theatre seats more than 1,300. It is also the perfect backdrop for everything from films to shows. This is largely due to the spatial relationship between the auditorium and the stage. Acoustics inside the building are outstanding.

The best design concept, however, is that it is fire-proof. How is this possible? It's simple, but clever. The boiler is housed separately from the theatre. It is located in the building next door, which is separated from the theatre by a two-foot thick firewall. Everything inside the building was also designed so as to be fireproof, from floors to fixtures. Even curtains!

The theatre opened on October 26, 1916. The first show was a comedy called 'Hit the Trail Holliday'. Patrons were awed by the floor-to-ceiling ivory-colored columns, private seating boxes, and 1,346 seats, including mezzanine seating. The mezzanine allows for seats above the stage level but below the balcony.

All kinds of performances have been held here

over the years, ranging from silent films to operas to magic shows—even the graduation ceremony for Decatur High School.

In April 1929, the first "talkies" came to the theatre. This is when the orchestra and band leader were let go since they were no longer needed. Back when movies were silent, the band played music to accompany suspense or action scenes. The first "talkies" that came to Lincoln Theatre were "Nothing but the Truth" starring Richard Dix and "Desert Song," a musical.

Here's a list of some late greats who have performed here:

Ethel Barrymore, actress (1917)

Al Jolson, singer (1917)

Jack Dempsey, heavyweight champion (1919)

John Philip Sousa and his band (1922)

Harry Blackstone, magician (1923)

Harry Houdini, magician (although there is some debate as to whether he actually performed here)

Bob Hope, actor (1929)

Horror movie stars: Bela Lugosi (1931) and Boris Karloff (1932)

The theatre was sold to Great States, a national theater chain, but Clarence Wait retained ownership of the building. It was inherited by his two brothers in 1936 upon his death. Six years later, a fire broke out in the next door drugstore. It took four hours to put out the fire, which destroyed a couple of neighboring buildings. But no damage was done to the fireproof theatre. Another fire occurred in 1960, but the theatre suffered no damage.

The building was sold in 1974 to Pitt Theaters, who bought out Great States. It was sold again a few months later and then closed in December 1980 when the owner of the building wouldn't renew the theater's lease.

It sat empty for many years until the early 1990s when a local preservation group was formed to preserve and maintain the historic property. Edward Wedelstedt gave the non-profit group the adjoining property in 1995, which allowed for further expansion of the theatre.

The Hauntings

Some believe that more than one ghost haunts this theatre. A popular theory is that the two men who died in the hotel fire haunt the property. A woman, possibly an actress who once performed here, reportedly haunts the theatre. An apparition wearing a long, flowing dress that may be a costume has been seen.

But the best known ghost is "Red." "Red" was a stagehand during the vaudeville days. His nickname came because of his bushy, red hair. He was good at his job and loved his work and the theatre. He was content to work there until his death, which happened one night when he fell off a seventy-five-foot high catwalk. It was a violent, gory death because he got caught on an apparatus which tore off his arm. His anguished screams were heard as the piece of equipment pierced his arm and claimed most of it before releasing the man to plunge the rest of the way to the stage. He was pronounced dead within a few minutes.

Another version of this tale is that "Red" only had one arm when he was hired. He lost it while serving in World War I. He died in his sleep while taking a mid-day nap in the theater before an evening performance. Regardless of which version you choose to believe, "Red" is one of the ghosts who haunt his beloved theatre.

It could be his footsteps that are heard or his whispers or screams that have been heard. The sound of a heavy stage curtain being pulled open or close has been heard by many when there is no logical reason for this noise.

Shadowy figures have been spotted in the balcony and on the staircase, but no one is found when the areas are investigated. In fact, the most haunted place in the theatre is the spiral staircase. Too many times to count, a figure has been seen and footsteps heard. Seats go up and down, as if someone is sitting down or standing up. Cold spots are often felt for no good reason and a few have reported being touched by an unseen presence.

Visitor Information

It looked like it might be lights out for Lincoln earlier this year due to significant financial and renovation issues. The doors were closed for a while and there was talk of the building being put up for sale. However, the show has gone on. The theatre reopened on April 28, 2012.

127 N. Main Street (downtown Decatur)

Decatur, IL 62523

www.lincolnsquaretheatre.com

It takes 3 hours (180 miles) to get to Decatur from Chicago, Illinois. The distance is 174 miles (3 hours) from Indianapolis, Indiana.

Terrance Zepke

Belcourt Castle

Belcourt Castle

FUN FACTS:

The library, which was added by Alva Belmont, has four secret doors.

The grand staircase is hand-carved, which took hundreds of European craftsmen three years to complete. Other noteworthy features include a huge Russian chandelier made with 13,000 crystal prisms. It is surrounded by eight smaller crystal chandeliers.

There is an oval Versailles dining room ceiling that is hand sculptured. French Empire style columns, mirrored doors, and mirrored shutters create a spectacular effect. When open, they overlook the ocean. Belcourt was completed in 1894 at a final cost of $3,000,000 ($74,614,478 in 2010 dollars).

The most haunted room is the ballroom and it is believed that there are a couple of cursed objects in the castle.

The History

This is a spectacular place to have such humble beginnings. The "Belcourt" began as a hunting lodge. The original plan called for one bedroom and one bathroom. There was no kitchen, but there was a huge stable and sleeping quarters for all the servants. Reportedly, he had thirty horses and thirty servants in the early days at Belcourt. His show and racing horses were given only the best. They each had comfortable stalls and slept on fine linens imported from Ireland.

Somehow this simple plan ballooned into a 50,000 square-foot edifice that included sixty rooms. It was designed by renowned architect Richard M. Hunt in a Louis XIII French Renaissance style and required 300 European craftsmen to build it. A kitchen was eventually built but not in the house as Oliver was terribly afraid that a fire might break out in the kitchen and destroy the home. He built the kitchen in another building and food was delivered by carriage to the main house. There are tunnels that extended from the house to the kitchen so that servants could easily go back and forth. It cost three million dollars and three and a half years to complete (1891 – 1894). The price tag is equivalent to over seventy million today. No wonder ghosts choose to linger here!

This may seem extravagant for a hunting retreat, but not to its owner. Oliver Belmont was born on November 12, 1858. His father was a banker and one of the richest men in the world. At 24, Oliver married Sara Swan Whiting but the pair divorced that same year! Sara gave birth to a baby girl soon after the divorce became final. Oliver never saw his daughter, who died in her 20s.

Oliver Hazard Perry Belmont inherited sixty million dollars in 1890, so money was no object. In addition to being very wealthy, the bachelor had many other appealing qualities. He was a graduate of Annapolis Naval Academy, had served one term as a Congressman, belonged to all the right social clubs, and had lots of interesting hobbies.

Oliver eventually remarried. Of all the women he could have had, Oliver ended up marrying his best friend's ex-wife, Anna Vanderbilt, less than one year after the divorce. She was responsible for many renovations in the house. Reportedly, she had the Grand Staircase moved four times before the workmen refused to do it anymore. When Oliver died in 1908, Anna threw herself into politics, especially women's' rights. It seemed she liked to live well too. At one point, she owned nine estates!

She chose her favorite for retirement, a chateau in France. She lived there until her death in 1933. She had a good life, living to a ripe old age of 80. She would have lived longer had she not suffered certain injuries during a carriage accident. She was buried next to Oliver in the Belmont family mausoleum in New York.

Oliver's nineteen-year-old nephew, August Belmont IV inherited Belcourt. But it ended up in the possession of Oliver's last surviving brother, who sold it in 1940. Belcourt was no longer in the Belmont family for the first time in its history. And it changed ownership several more times until 1956 when it was bought by Harold B. Tinney. The Tinney family drove by the vacant mansion and knew immediately that they wanted it. They bought it at the bargain price of $25,000.

The following year it became Belcourt Castle and a public museum. The Tinney family appreciated the beauty of the mansion. They made many renovations to the rundown property and delighted in furnishing it with spectacular antiques and works of art from nearly three dozen countries.

His son, Donald, was married at Belcourt Castle in 1960. He met his bride there when she was a student working as a tour guide one summer. The property remains in the Tinney family after being involved in a lengthy legal battle between the Tinney family and

Ruth Tinney's handyman, Kevin Koellisch, who laid claim to the property."

The Hauntings

There seem to be three items in the chateau that draw paranormal activity. One is a statue. It is a monk wearing a brown robe. Wherever it is placed inside the house, a figure wearing a brown robe is sometimes seen nearby. This happened repeatedly until the status was moved to the chapel. After that, the figure was never seen again.

The other items are two salt chairs. Salt chairs were made for and used only by kings. There was a storage compartment underneath the seat. Salt was a valuable commodity in those days, more valuable than gold or silver. The seat flipped up, revealing a prized salt stash. Any man that has tried to sit in one of these chairs has experienced a weird feeling, as if someone were already seated. One man was even expelled from the chair by an unseen presence. Since no one has been allowed to sit in one of these valuable antiques in a long time, there has been no ghostly documentation in a long time.

The most haunted room is the ballroom. It is also one of the loveliest rooms complete with a huge castle fireplace and 13th century stained glass. But what is remembered most is not the design or items in the room but the seemingly paranormal activity. Visitors, employees, family members, and guests have seen strange shadows in one corner of the French gothic style ballroom. Furniture and objects have been moved, cold spots are often felt, especially near two salt chairs, footsteps and strange sounds are heard when no one is present. There are several pieces of armor that have been seen moving or have been found in another room with no one claiming responsibility for moving the armor.

The Tinney family dog refused to enter the ballroom. Mrs. Tinney has heard screams coming from inside the room on occasion but never found anyone when she ran into the room to investigate. She sometimes found the lights shortly after she knew she had turned them off for the night. Some visitors claim to have felt physically sick until they exited the room.

Some believe the paranormal activity is not from the spirits of former owners but rather from cursed objects. Since the antiques and artwork have been collected from all over the world, some believe that some of the pieces might be haunted. For example, one of the suits of armor was worn by a gentleman who was killed when a spear stabbed him in the eye. It is believed that his cry of anguish is the scream that is sometimes heard by Mrs. Tinney. Most of the armor dates back to Oliver Belmont. One of his hobbies was collecting armor.

Visitor Information

657 Bellevue Avenue

Newport, Rhode Island 02840

www.belcourtcastle.com

The Tinney family sold Belcourt to Alex and Ani Jewelry Company founder, Carolyn Rafaelian, a few years ago. She has restored the mansion and continues to offer tours, weddings, and other social/charitable events on site.

It is a fifty-minute drive (35 miles) from Providence, Rhode Island. From Hartford, Connecticut it is ninety-five miles (2 hours). It takes four hours (190 miles) to reach Newport from New York City.

St. Louis Cemetery #1

St. Louis Cemetery #1

The History

This is one of three cemeteries that make up the St. Louis Cemetery. It is also the oldest surviving cemetery in New Orleans, dating back to 1789, which makes it historically important. This explains why it is on the National Register of Historic Places. It has survived floods, fires, neglect, and vandalism.

St. Louis Cemetery was built to replace St. Peter Cemetery, which no longer exists. The graves are all built above ground because the city is below sea level. Visitors will note that the few existing old slab graves have been weighted down with bricks so that the coffin does not pop up out of the ground.

A fire, yellow fever epidemic, and a flood in the late 1800s resulted in so many deaths that bodies were often lying around for days waiting for graves to be dug. According to legend, grave diggers stayed intoxicated so as to tolerate the stench from the decaying bodies.

Interestingly, during the immense flooding that followed Hurricane Katrina, the cemetery remained unscathed. No tombs were damaged. The only indication of the legendary flood is the waterline marks that can be seen on most tombs.

All these grand tombs all over New Orleans are the reason for the nickname "Cities of the Dead." The vaults vary according to affluence. Some are quite simple while others are very ornate. Some are very small and some big enough to accommodate a large family. Some family tombs look like cute little houses surrounded by iron fences. You may hear folks refer to the tombs as "ovens" because many of them are shaped so as to resemble brick ovens.

At the back of the cemetery is "pauper's field." This is a large area with unmarked graves for folks who couldn't afford to buy a vault. Even those who could not afford a vault could usually find a family who would allow them to be added to their vault rather than being buried in an unmarked grave.

Tombs are generally constructed of brick and covered with stucco or plaster. They are usually parapet or platform tombs. Their conditions vary from derelict to good, depending on upkeep and restoration efforts. Vaults could be valuable and as such were deeded in wills and sold during tough financial times. Or the tombs were stolen by unscrupulous people. A man named Henry Vignes had the deed to his family's vault. He left the papers with his landlady when he went to sea, trusting her to keep them safe. Instead, she sold the vault and made a tidy sum. When Henry came home, he discovered that he no longer owned the vault. Sadly, he died before the matter could be resolved. He was buried in the pauper's field in an unmarked grave.

Since this is a Roman Catholic cemetery, Catholic were buried in the main part and Jews and Protestants were buried in the back of the cemetery. One of the most distinguishing things about the cemetery is the many alleys and paths that wind through and around all the vaults. They vary from tiny alleys to wide pathways.

Located on the edge of the French Quarter, it accommodates more than 600 tombs, including many notable citizens. Here are a few of the distinguished persons found here:

Paul Morphy: world champion chess player

Group vault for men who died during the Battle of New Orleans

Etienne de Bore´: first mayor of New Orleans and successful entrepreneur

Bernard de Marigny: served on New Orleans City Council and as President of Louisiana Senate. He was also a serious gambler who is credited with bringing the game of craps to New Orleans. He gambled all his money away and had to sell off his plantation, eventually dying a pauper

Bert Brigand Lagon: former city planner for New Orleans who later became a pirate who joined up with the famous Jean Lafitte

But there is no doubt that the most infamous inhabitant of this cemetery is Voodoo Priestess Marie Laveau. She was conceived when a plantation owner and a Creole woman had a brief affair. She married when she was barely eighteen years old, anxious to start a better life. She married a Haitian man, who introduced her to voodoo (called Santeri in Haiti).
She worked as a hairdresser and helped with the

afflicted during several epidemics. She had a daughter, whom she also named Marie. She taught her daughter everything she knew about voodoo. Both women had quite a following. So much so that when the older Marie died, she was not allowed to be buried in the family vault. Authorities feared that her followers would besiege the cemetery, so she was buried in an unmarked grave.

Oddly, the same authorities allowed her daughter, Marie Deux, to be buried in the family vault. Perhaps they realized that they had no legal right to stop it. Or maybe they were fearful of retribution by the priestess and her followers.

The Hauntings

The spirits of the people discussed in this chapter are who many believe haunts the cemetery. These people have been seen by visitors and have been reported to appear more like human beings than as apparitions. The spirit of Henry Vignes sometimes appears during a funeral and is known to approach visitors and asks for help finding the Vignes family vault.

Many believe that Marie Laveau and her daughter haunt the cemetery. The mother may haunt it because she was not buried properly in the family vault. The daughter might be conflicted over her Roman

Catholic religion and the black magic she practiced. Her figure has been seen on a path near her family vault. She has cursed visitors but does not follow when they turn away.

The spirit of a man named Alphonse has been known to touch visitors. He extends an icy hand either on a shoulder or when he grips a visitor's hand in greeting before disappearing. He always disappears after making contact. He is seen on occasion bringing flowers to graves.

Investigations have shown shadowy figures and orbs in photographs and strange EVPs have been recorded. One recording reveals "I need to rest!"

Visitor Information

The cemetery sits on the peripheral of the French Quarter. It is not advisable to wear expensive jewelry or carry cash, and be aware of your surroundings. The cemetery, which is located just eight blocks from the Mississippi River, is owned and maintained by the Archdiocese of New Orleans. A non-profit group, Save Our Cemeteries, offers daily tours and is only way to explore this old cemetery. If you are not accompanied by a licensed guide, you will not be allowed to enter the premises.

http://www.saveourcemeteries.org/st-louis-cemetery-no-1-tour/

A long-time tradition for many visitors, albeit this is a form of vandalism, is to knock three times on front of Marie's tomb, leave an "XXX" in chalk (you'll see where others have done this), and knock again three times, it is said that whatever you wish will come true—if you also leave an offering, such as flowers, candles, charms, and coins. You'll see where many others have done this ritual.

The removal (or even moving) of objects inside a New Orleans cemetery is punishable by law. This is considered a serious offense and witnesses are encouraged to call the authorities. Visitors are asked to be respectful of the dead when inside the cemetery and not to litter or act inappropriately.

425 Basin Street (Basin and St. Louis Streets)
New Orleans, Louisiana 70112

From Baton Rouge, Louisiana it is eighty miles (1 hour, 20 minutes) to New Orleans. It takes 7.5 hours (444 miles) to get to NO from Little Rock, Arkansas and 13 hours (822 miles) from Myrtle Beach, South Carolina.

Note: St. Louis Cemetery #2 is three blocks from here on Clairbourne Avenue and St. Louis Cemetery #3 is two miles away on Esplanada Avenue. #1 and #2 are on the African American Heritage Trail. St. Louis #3 was built in 1854 and visitors will notice that the vaults are more grandiose than the other two St. Louis cemeteries.

Terrance Zepke

Stone's Public House

Stone's Public House

FUN FACTS:

This place is haunted by several ghosts.

It was a stop on the Underground Railroad.

There was at least one death and one secret murder on this property.

The History

John Stone was a farmer, landowner, captain in the militia, and businessman. He pursued all these occupations because he could never pass up an opportunity to make money. When Stone heard that the railroad was coming to town, he decided to open a hotel. The railroad would be built in the center of town on land he owned, so that made the location of the hotel a no brainer. It was built within few feet of the railroad tracks.

Construction began in 1832 and the hotel opened on September 20, 1834. He had a barn and house built on the site too. The shrewd businessman ran the inn for two years. After he had made a success of the business, he leased it to various innkeepers for more than twenty years. However, he continued to live in the house he had built nearby.

Stone died in 1858 and W.A. Scott bought the business ten years later. It changed ownership several times during 1968 – 1976. It became rundown and may have ended up demolished if not for "Cappy" Fournier. Fournier bought the building in 1976 and made extensive repairs. He also renamed it John Stone's Inn. In 2003, it was renamed Stone's Public House by owner Matt Murphy. The name change was logical given that it no longer offered lodging.

The Hauntings

There's another reason that the owner changed the name. He received lots of calls from folks wanting to stay at the haunted inn. He got tired of having to repeatedly explain that while the name certainly suggested it offered lodging, the property was now a restaurant.

Some patrons claim they get a creepy sensation when they look at John Stone's portrait. Those claims certainly aren't enough to say a place is haunted, but what about all the other things that have happened over the years that defy logical explanation?

Paranormal activity dates back to Leonard "Cappy" Fournier. So many strange things happened that he consulted a psychic. He explained to the psychic that there are locked doors that swing open and lights go on and off for no good reason. Glasses fly into the air and shatter onto the floor when there is no wind or anyone near the glasses. Disembodied voices have been heard. Bar staff have complained of hearing male and female voices late at night when they are doing their closing duties. But they know they are alone or that the only other employee is elsewhere in the building.

Some employees and patrons have felt a hand on their necks or a tap on their shoulders, but turn to find no one is there. Bartenders often turn around to find water running in the little sink.

The most haunted area in the house is the "function room" upstairs. Most folks, including the psychic, have told Fournier that they get a really weird feeling in that room, especially in the back part of the room.

So what did the psychic have to say? Actually, more than one psychic has been brought here. All agree that there is more than one spirit lingering at Stone's Public House. Who these spirits are remains a mystery. It is believed that one is the spirit of a man named Burt Philips who died inside the inn during the 1890s.

One psychic claims to have at least some of the answers. After communicating with some spirits, including a chambermaid named Sadie, he learned that John Stone killed a guest at The Railroad House. A New York native salesman named Michael was lodging at the inn for an extended period of time. Stone liked the young man. He invited him to join his group for a friendly card game.

Things went south when Michael kept winning.

When he was up almost $3,000, Stone accused him of cheating. Irate, he hit the man over the head with the butt of his gun. He only meant to injure the man, but the blow was fatal. There were five people who witnessed the killing. After some discussion, they came up with a plan. They were sworn to secrecy, which wasn't hard since no one wanted to explain his involvement. The men helped Stone get the body to the basement to hide it. Sadie the maid saw the men carrying the corpse down to the basement, but never told anyone for fear of losing her job or getting killed too.

The psychic believes that the spirit of Sadie, Michael, and the six participants in the card game still haunt the place.

But there is at least one more ghost. This one is the spirit of a little girl who died a tragic death. She was the niece of an employee of the inn. She became very ill and ultimately died in a room on the second floor of the inn. Some believe she is still here, at least in spirit. A few people who had never heard the story have said they have seen a little girl looking out the second floor window. Confused, they ask an employee or manager because they thought that no one stays at the old inn anymore. Sometimes noises are heard coming from that room, but nothing and no one is ever found when someone investigates the sightings or sounds.

But that may not be all the ghosts at Stone's Public House. A hidden room was discovered in the basement many years ago. It turns out that the property was a "station" on the Underground Railroad. A cot, blankets, lantern, and water barrel were found in the hidden room. It's possible that the spirits of runaway slaves haunt this place.

Visitor Information

The restaurant is open to the public every day except Mondays.

179 Main Street. Ashland, Massachusetts 01721.
www.stonespublichouse.com

Ashland is 26 miles from Boston, Massachusetts. It is 7 hours and 11 minutes (380 miles) from Newark, New Jersey or from Baltimore, Maryland to Ashland.

Tombstone

Tombstone

FUN FACTS:

During its heyday, there were 106 saloons in Tombstone, but the Bird Cage was considered one of the best of those found in the Red Light District. On the main level there was a gambling area and bar. There were "cribs" (small rooms) located upstairs. Actually, the cribs were suspended over each side of the large gambling hall. As such, they had no doors. There were curtains that were drawn when prostitutes were "entertaining." At one time, there were more than 3,000 prostitutes in Tombstone.

According to *Guinness Book of World Records*, the world's largest rosebush was planted in Tombstone in 1885 and still exists. This Lady Banksia rose now covers 8,000 square feet of the roof on the Rose Tree Inn Museum, and has a trunk width of twelve feet!

There are more than 140 bullet holes inside the Bird Cage Theatre that occurred during gambling and drinking disputes. Twenty-six people died inside the building. According to records, $20 would buy a patron a good bottle of whiskey and a prostitute for the night.

The History

Tombstone was settled in 1877 by a man named Ed Schieffelin. Soldiers who came across the prospector while they were on the lookout for Apache Indians thought he was a fool. They laughingly told him that "the only stone he'll find out there will be his tombstone." This was a warning that the man was crazy for venturing high up into those hills of the southeast Arizona Territory that was known to be infested with Apache Indians. But Schieffelin found a silver mine. Remembering what the soldiers had said, he called it 'Tombstone'.

Once word spread about Schieffelin's discovery, everyone from cowboys to lawyers came to 'Tombstone' in search of wealth. By the late 1880s, the population had swelled to more than 7,500. However, this is not an accurate figure given that it only takes into account registered Caucasian men who were over the age of twenty-one. But many of the men were under the age of 21, not to mention all the Chinese and Mexican men, women, and children. The population was probably closer to 12,000 - 20,000. It was an interesting demographic that comprised Tombstone. There were wealthy businessmen, cowboys, prostitutes, and immigrant workers.

In fact, Tombstone was the fastest growing city

between St. Louis, Missouri and San Francisco, California in the late 1800s. The town was full of restaurants, schools, churches, and other businesses, including a newspaper and approximately 100 saloons. The first public swimming pool in Arizona opened here.

But Tombstone's claim to fame was the theater. Two of the most famous were the Bird Cage Theatre and Schieffelin Hall. The latter opened in 1881 and was where the refined folks went for entertainment. It was built by Al Schieffelin, who was town founder Ed Schieffelin's brother. It is the biggest adobe building in the southwestern United States. In addition to a theater, it was used as a meeting place and recital hall. It is still used as a meeting place by local groups and government.

To the contrary, the Bird Cage Theatre was where the cowboys and prospectors went for entertainment. The building housed a theater, saloon, gambling room, and brothel. The Bird Cage Theatre was always open for business, even on Christmas Day.

It was open 24/7 until it shut down in 1889. In the basement there was a poker game that never ended. The cost was $1,000 for a buy-in so it was a high-stakes game for serious gamblers only, such as Randolph Hearst, Adolph Busch, and Doc Holliday. Reportedly, the game ran for eight years, five months, and three days!

According to one newspaper, "The Bird Cage Theatre is the wildest, wickedest night spot between Basin Street and the Barbary Coast." Respectable women citizens of Tombstone refused to walk past the front of the building. Instead, they crossed the street and then crossed back again after passing the place of ill repute.

A business license was granted to "Dutch Annie" Smith in 1881 to run a "House of Ill Fame." That document is still hanging on the wall. The place re-opened in 1934 and remains a tourist attraction today. The poker room is said to look exactly the same as it did during the years the Birdcage was in operation.

Given Tombstone's reputation, it is no wonder that a cemetery had to be built. Boothill Graveyard was used from 1879 until 1884. Due to overcrowding and neglect, a new cemetery had to be built, Tombstone City Cemetery. Additionally, respectable citizens didn't want to be buried next to gunfighters and cowboys.

Boothill Cemetery (also known as 'The Old Cemetery') got its name because so many men died with their boots on during gunfights or during gambling disputes. Grave markers often reflect how the men died, such as "Hanged by Mistake" and "Murdered on the Streets of Tombstone." Approximately 250 are buried in this historical graveyard.

In addition to Boothill Cemetery, Bird Cage Theatre, Big-nosed Kate's Saloon, tourists flock to Tombstone to see the OK Corral. This is where the famous gunfight between the Earps and the Clanton-McLaury gang took place. On October 26, 1881, the infamous clash between the cowboys and the lawmen lasted less than a minute. During that time, nearly three dozen shots were fired. Remember that these are some of the fastest gunmen in the West. Bill Clanton, Tom McLaury, and Frank McLaury died during that shootout. Virgil Earp and Morgan Earp were wounded. Wyatt Earp and Doc Holliday didn't even suffer a scratch. The area where this famous gunfight took place is reportedly haunted.

Over the years, more than $37 million worth of silver ore was mined in the Tombstone area. Eventually, most of the silver (and some gold) had been mined that could be accessed. Attempts were made to go below 500 feet, but that resulted in flooded mines. The water was pumped out but became too costly to continue this practice. Once there was no more mining, many packed up and left. By the 1930s, Tombstone's population was less than 150.

Nowadays, the population holds steady at roughly 1,500. Most of the residents work in the tourism industry.

The Hauntings

Most of the small town of Tombstone is haunted, including Boothill Cemetery, Big-Nosed Kate's Saloon, and the Bird Cage Theatre.

Who haunts these places? Impossible to say given all the deaths that have transpired here. For example, there were twenty-six murders inside the **Bird Cage Theatre** and we only know a few specifics. One of the most notorious murders was committed by a prostitute named Gold Dollar.

Most of the prostitutes had regular clients. One of Gold Dollar's regulars was Billy Milgreen. The prospector usually showed up when he had claim money in his pocket. On this night, another prostitute began flirting with him while he waited on Gold Dollar. When Gold Dollar appeared and discovered Margarita all over one of her favorite clients, she became furious. She ran up to the woman who was sitting in Milgreen's lap, laughing and stroking his hair, and stabbed Margarita in the chest with a stiletto knife.

The bleeding woman fell out of the man's lap onto the floor. She swung the blade again as the woman tried to stand up. A crowd gathered, some of the other prostitutes screamed as they witnessed the attack, some of the men cheered while others tried to stop Gold Dollar. The sheriff was summoned. Realizing what she had done, Gold Dollar ran out of the building.

By the time the sheriff arrived, she was long gone. She was later captured, but the stiletto knife was never found. No one would testify, so she was released. Remarkably, the knife was found behind the theater many, many years later. It is on display, along with a plaque detailing the story.

A little boy died of Yellow Fever. He was believed to be the child of one of the prostitutes. His spirit is still seen on occasion. A stagehand was killed when a heavy sandbag fell several feet, landing on top of him. A ghostly apparition carrying a clipboard has been seen walking across the stage.

So it is no surprise that the spirits of prostitutes and men dressed like cowboys have been seen inside the building. Visitors have been tickled, pinched, and pushed by unseen forces. Also, visitors smell cigar smoke, perfume, and whiskey, especially during the morning hours. Smoking is not permitted in the building nowadays and the smell of perfume and whiskey permeate even when no one is drinking or wearing perfume. The sounds of music, laughter, shouting, and cursing have been heard late at night inside the building even though it is closed and there is no one inside.

The music has been determined to be the museum's sound system but no one knows how it gets turned on. There is no explanation for the laughter, shouting, talking, cursing, sounds of cards being shuffled, dice being thrown, and glasses clinking.

A former museum manager believes the place is haunted but is not afraid of the ghosts. She says they seem harmless. Sometimes objects have been moved from their location at closing time, such as gaming tables and poker chips. One example is a replica of Wyatt Earp. The figure has been placed in one of the balcony boxes looking out over the theatre. He has been found facing the other direction and his hat was always found on the floor below. When the figure was moved to another box (He had mistakenly been placed in the box the Clanton gang used to reserve and was moved to the box that had been his), the hat was never again found on the floor or the figure facing the opposite direction.

A school was built across from the theater in 1921. Students, teachers, and others who pass by the theater on a regular basis have reported unusual activity.

The most common thing reported is the sounds of loud partying and ruckus. Since the building is now vacant, these incidents were reported to local law enforcement. When authorities investigate, they expect to find teenagers or vandals or trespassers looking for a party spot, but they never find anyone there.

By the mid-1930s, the building was bought and reopened as a tourist attraction. Ghost groups have found that supernatural activity tends to take place most often after 9 p.m. Most employees do not like to be in the building after that time, even though the ghosts have never harmed anyone.

A theatre manager, Bill Hunley, has heard the sounds of boots walking across the floor, but never finds anyone there. He often smells stale cigar smoke. Occasionally, a woman's face appears in the mirror in photos but never before the 11th or 12th shot. The most common complaint is the sound of partying going on inside when the building is closed and there is no activity going on.

A ghost group conducted an official investigation in 2008 and caught a creepy image on film. SyFy Channel's 'Fact or Faked' investigated and debunked the photo. They came to the conclusion that the light, angle, and objects in front of the wall contributed to it being mistaken for a paranormal picture.

However, they spent a night doing their own investigation and had some paranormal encounters. A team member heard floorboards creak behind him but there was no one there. A full spectrum camera and light was left in one of the most haunted areas in the old theatre. It was a room that once belonged to a prostitute named Sadie Jo, who many believe still lays claim to the room. The crew found the camera turned off and moved outside of the room where it had been left. One team member captured a female voice on EVP. He asked "Is anyone here?" and the EVP picked up "We were!"

Another haunted locale is **Boothill Graveyard**. According to tombstones, roughly 250 men died in gunfights. Some of the cowboys who took part in the historic gunfight at the OK Corral are also buried here. Visitors to the cemetery have seen the ghosts of these men. Some report strange lights and sounds.

Big-nosed Kate's Saloon is another haunted site in Tombstone. The saloon began as The Grand Hotel, which opened its doors on September 9, 1880. The sixteen-room hotel was considered to be one of the best hotels in the state. Some of its most infamous guests include Wyatt Earp, Doc Holliday, and Ike Clanton. In fact, some of the Clanton-McLaury gang stayed here on

October 25, 1881—the night before the famous shootout at the OK Corral.

Sadly, a fire broke out on May 25, 1882. Less than two years after its grand opening, most of the building was destroyed. The place was rebuilt and became home to Big Nose Kate's Saloon. Katherine Elder was the first prostitute in Tombstone. She came to be known as "Big-nosed Kate" and was famous for her relationship with Doc Holliday. Some say she was his wife while others believe she was his common law wife, but that they were never legally married. One thing's for sure. They lived their lives on their own terms. He continued gambling and being a gunfighter until he died. Kate continued to be a prostitute, even while she was with Doc Holliday. One thing that isn't disputed is that she helped him escape from a jail in Fort Griffin, Texas.

Big-nosed Kate was not only a tough lady, but a savvy businesswoman. She ran a profitable saloon and brothel in a city that was not only one of the most dangerous places in America at that time, but also a town full of similar businesses.

During its brief years as the Grand Hotel, a prospector named "Swamper" frequented the establishment. In exchange for his small room in the basement, he served as the property's handyman. While he worked at the hotel doing repairs and maintenance during the day, he spent most nights digging a tunnel from his room to one of the silver mines.

The saloon is located on Allen Street. The main bar is on the ground floor and there is a gift shop in the basement. If you go downstairs, you can see the tunnel that Swamper dug to a nearby mine shaft. This is also the most haunted area. Visitors have experienced ghostly encounters, especially early in the morning. It is generally believed to be haunted by Swamper. After years of digging and searching, Swamper found silver. Excited over his newfound wealth, he bragged about it one night. Soon afterwards, he was found murdered. Visitors have had their ankles grabbed and yanked when they get to the bottom of the basement steps. Some have seen a scary-looking figure in the basement pointing a finger, warning them to leave.

A female apparition has also been seen, although it is generally not believed to be Kate. The reason being that she is wearing a flowing dress (Kate seldom wore anything but pants). She may be the spirit of one of the prostitutes who worked for Kate.

A ghost who has been dubbed "Felix" also haunts the place. Descriptions of Felix always have him wearing clothing from the 1800s, including a long sleeve shirt. He roams the halls and if approached will disappear.

In addition to these sightings, heavy footsteps are heard, glasses are thrown into the air (so often that bartenders have to keep a written list), trash can lids fly off the cans and roll across the floor, and doors open by themselves. Some visitors have taken photos of the animated mannequins only to be told later that the mannequins are not animated. Waitresses have complained of their skirts being tugged, hair pulled, and their pens removed from their pockets.

Visitor Information

Tombstone, dubbed "The Town Too Tough to Die," is seventy miles southeast of Tucson. For more information and directions, visit www.townoftombstone.com

Birdcage Theater is at 535 East Allen Street and is open to the public. www.tombstonebirdcage.com. Both self-guided and nightly ghost tours are offered.

Boothill Cemetery is on the edge of town and open to the public. It is free but donations are accepted.

Admission is charged to enter the OK Corral but part of it can be seen free of charge.

Big-nosed Kate's Saloon is a restaurant, gift shop, and saloon that is open to the public. It is located in the heart of town at 417 E. Allen Street. www.bignosekate.com

It is 1,250 miles to get from Rapid City, South Dakota to Tombstone. From Tucson, it is a short 1 hour and twelve minute drive (72 miles). From Denver, Colorado it is 870 miles (13 hours).

Queen Mary

Queen Mary

FUN FACTS:

The *Queen Mary* was used during World War II. The ship carried more than 800,000 troops and made thirteen trips that became known as the "bride and baby" voyages in 1946 to bring 22,000 war brides and their children to the U.S. and Canada.

After the war and more than 1,000 transatlantic voyages, the *Queen Mary* was sold in 1967. It became a museum, hotel, and tourist attraction. It is moored in Long Beach, California.

Royalty and celebrities have sailed on the grand *Queen Mary*, including The Duke and Duchess of Windsor, Sir Winston Churchill (with 5,000 German prisoners of war), Greta Garbo, George Gershwin, Mary Pickford, and Clark Gable.

The History

The idea for the spectacular ship was born in 1929 and work began on the 1,000-foot vessel the following year. Work halted between 1931 – 1934 due to the Great Depression and a lack of funding. Cunard Steamship Company merged with White Star Line (the same company that owned *Titanic*), so financing was available to continue with the project. It also meant that White Star was responsible for overseeing the ship building.

The *Queen Mary* was much bigger than *Titanic*. Weighing in at 81,237 gross tons, the nine-story, twelve-deck vessel was finally completed in 1936. She made her maiden voyage on May 27, 1936. Before her departure, she was visited by many dignitaries, including King Edward VIII, Princess Elizabeth, the Duke and Duchess of Kent, the Duchess of Gloucester, the Duke and Duchess of York, and Her Majesty Queen Mary.

For three years, the *HMS Queen Mary* made transatlantic crossings and catered to its affluent passengers. But when WWII broke out in 1939, the ship was commandeered by the military. It was repainted a dull grey, which earned it the nickname "The Grey Ghost."

It now carried well over 5,000 people whereas its maximum capacity as a cruise ship had been 2,400. In fact, she set a record for carrying the most people—16,683. The *Queen Mary* participated in nearly every major campaign, including D-Day. The vessel had logged 600,000 miles by the end of the war.

The ship reverted to its original purpose in 1947.

Transatlantic voyages continued between England and New York until the early 1960s. They lost favor when air travel became readily available and affordable for everyone. Cunard abandoned transatlantic crossings and began offering Caribbean cruises, but the ship lacked amenities to compete with other cruise ships. Pools and air conditioning weren't needed for transatlantic trips but were essential for Caribbean cruises.

In April 1966, the ship was put up for sale. The following year the *Queen Mary* was sold for $3.45 million to the city of Long Beach, California, who wanted it to attract tourism. On December 9, 1967, she made one last voyage. The ship sailed into Long Beach where it has been moored ever since.

The Hauntings

There have been as many as forty-nine documented deaths on the ship. Some say there are as many as 150 ghosts on board. One psychic puts the number much higher. The most paranormal activity has been reported in the engine room and swimming pools.

The engine room's famed "Door 13" was featured in the hit movie, *Poseidon Adventure*. Door 13 crushed two men to death on two separate occasions. One of the men, John Peddler, was just eighteen years old. His spirit has been seen wearing what the young man was wearing during the deadly drill—blue overalls. He is seen walking along Shaft Alley before disappearing at Door 13.

There were two swimming pools for the first and second-class passengers. Women wearing old-fashioned bathing suits are still seen wandering around the first-class passenger pool. The sounds of water splashing and wet footprints are seen when there is no water in the pool. In the area where the second-class passenger pool once stood (now the theater) the spirit of a little girl has been encountered. Jackie drowned many years ago during a voyage, but she is still seen and heard. The sounds of a little girl laughing and whispering have been heard by ghost detecting EVPs.

The Queen's Salon was once the first class lounge. A pretty young lady wearing a white ball gown is sometimes seen dancing in the corner of the room. Also, a dark-haired man has been seen in some of the first-class staterooms wearing a 1930s era suit. Lights sometimes come on, cabin telephones ring, and the water gushes out of the faucet during the wee hours of the morning, but maintenance can find no electrical or mechanical reason for these events. The most haunted guest room is the Sir Winston Churchill Suite. Guests come back to the room to find the smell of cigar. They also say they have heard someone clearing his throat and thumping sounds.

Throughout the ship, doors are heard slamming, knocking on the doors, clanging of metal, cries, footsteps, muffled voices, laughter, and other unexplainable noises are heard when no one is there. Some guests claim that their bed sheets were pulled off during the night by an unseen presence.

Cold spots are inexplicably felt in several places on the ship. Complaints of cigarette and pipe smoke are made but no evidence of smoking is found and smoking is not permitted anywhere on the ship.

While hundreds of amateur and professional ghost hunters have investigated the ship over the years, one of the most famous investigators is Psychic Peter James from the television show, 'Sightings'. He has spent nearly twenty years visiting the ship while giving ghost tours and believes it to be one of the most haunted places in the world. He claims there are as many as 600 active ghosts on board!

He says many are the spirits of deceased sailors. Some are men who died of heat stroke during the war. There was no air conditioning and there were thousands of men crammed on board and they were stationed in the Indian Ocean for an extended period of time. Also, some prisoners-of-war committed suicide while being held on board. Many of the POWs were only 17 – 19, much too young to handle their situation. In a collision with another ship, as many as 300 men died in 1942.

There were also numerous deaths on board while the *Queen Mary* was a cruise ship, such as drowning, heart attacks, fatal accidents, and other medical problems that resulted in death.

Psychic Peter James says that he has spoken with Jackie. He says she is five years old and spoke of "the other pool." He was confused until he realized that the theater was once the second-class swimming pool. He says that he has also communicated with an angry spirit named Sarah, who also drowned in this pool.

Another ghost tour leader, Erika Frost, has communicated with several ghosts, including the young seaman crushed by Door 13. She warns participants they may feel cold, nauseas, or dizzy during the tour as this often happens.

Visitor Information

Close to 1.5 million people visit the *Queen Mary* each year. The ship, which is listed on the National Register of Historic Places, features fourteen Art Deco salons, spa, restaurants, shops, and exhibits. Visitors can choose from many options, such as day tours, night tours, ghost tours, dining in one of its fine restaurants, visiting its spa and shops, or staying overnight. The ship has been made into a hotel so anyone can make a reservation to stay in one of its guest rooms or suites aboard the haunted ship—if you dare!

Some tips:

Plan on doing a lot of walking so wear comfortable shoes and clothing. It takes at least 3-4 hours to properly tour the ship.

Not all areas are handicap accessible. Climbing stairs is required in certain areas.

You need your own flashlight if coming for a night tour.

The ghost tour is not recommended for anyone under fifteen years old. There is a **Ghosts & Legends Show** described as "in this spooky and fun, interactive, special effects adventure." http://www.queenmary.com/tours-exhibits/tours-exhibits-attractions/ghost-and-legends/

1126 Queens Highway

Long Beach, California 90802

www.queenmary.com

From Dallas, Texas it is a 21.5 hour drive (1,445 miles). It is 2,050 miles (30.5 hours) from Birmingham, Alabama. From Santa Barbara, California to Long Beach is a short two-hour drive.

Timeline

Ship construction took place from 1930 – 1936.

Maiden voyage was in 1936.

Ship used by military from 1939 – 1946.

Queen Mary reverts to being cruise ship in 1947.

Queen Mary is put up for sale in 1966.

Queen Mary is sold to City of Long Beach for $3.45 million in the summer of 1967.

Last transatlantic voyage was during September 1967.

Queen Mary arrives in Long Beach, CA on December 9, 1967.

Ship is taken off the British registry and officially turned over to the City of Long Beach on December 11, 1967

The ship opened as a hotel and attraction on November 2, 1972.

After several changes of ownership and management, the *Queen Mary* closes in 1992, but reopens the following year.

The last captain of the vessel, Captain John T. Jones, dies at age 87 in May 1993.

Terrance Zepke

Ohio State Reformatory

Ohio State Reformatory (Mansfield Reformatory)

FUN FACTS:

The prison has been featured in several big Hollywood movies, such as Shawshank Redemption, Air Force One, and Tango and Cash.

Warden Cardwell let 150 exemplary prisoners attend the Ohio State Fair in 1969. They were allowed to go unrestrained and without supervision wherever they wanted. There were no incidents so the next year prisoners were allowed to return to the state fair and did so without incident.

There have been numerous escape attempts over the years. The last one was in 1952 when nine men sawed their way out of their dormitory. Seven were soon caught, but the other two got away.

The History

This 250,000-square-foot edifice is the world's largest free-standing cell block. It was purposely named a reformatory rather than a prison.

Construction began in November 1886 and took ten years before the project was completed. The cost of the facility was $93,370.50, which doesn't include inmate labor. The architecture design is a combination of Gothic, Queen Anne, and Romanesque, designed by noted architect Levi T. Scofield. It wasn't until September 1896 that the first inmates arrived at OSR.

The prison, which held men and women, housed more than 150,000 inmates during its close to 100 years in operation. Eleven cells were built just for women prisoners. Women weren't sent here after 1916 when the Ohio Reformatory for Women was built in Marysville.

There were some notable prisoners. One was William Sidney Porter, an inmate who spent a lot of time writing stories, which he later published under the pen name "O. Henry." Dave Blackburn was an inmate who was also an inventor. He invented the dishwasher and several life-saving devices. Gates Brown went on to play for the Detroit Tigers after his incarceration. Prisoner Henry Baker was a member of the famed Brinks Gang. Running back for the Cleveland Browns, Kevin Mack, served a brief sentence for drug charges. Confederate Army General John Hunt Morgan served time here as a prisoner of war after being captured in 1863. He and his men escaped in the fall of 1863 by tunneling their way out.

Visitors will notice that there are 215 grave markers, which means that some inmates never left.

Some were killed during deadly prison assaults while others died of disease, such as the flu and TB. Some desperate men took their own lives. One man hanged himself and another set himself on fire using turpentine and paint thinner he had stolen from the prison furniture shop.

Once becoming an inmate at OSR, prisoners were no longer referred to by name, but were assigned a number. Even the inmates who died and were buried here had numbers, not names, on their grave markers.

Some freed prisoners ended up back at OSR. In July 1948, two prisoners out on parole sought revenge by killing Superintendent John Niebel, his wife, and daughter. They fled after committing the gruesome crimes. After an exhaustive manhunt that spanned six states, the men were found. There was a shootout that resulted in the arrest of Robert Daniels and the death of James West. Daniels would have been better off if he had died during the shootout since he was executed on January 3, 1949.

Less than one year later, there was more tragedy at OSR. While the warden's wife, Helen, was removing a box from a closet shelf, a concealed gun was accidentally disturbed and discharged. The stray bullet hit the woman and she died the next day as a result of the wound. According to some, this never happened. Some believe Warden Glattke wanted out of the marriage but didn't want the ordeal or scandal of a divorce. So, he killed his wife or may have hired someone to do it and made up the story to conceal the murder. Some suggest that Helen took her own life to escape an unhappy marriage. But what really happened will never be known since the warden died of a heart attack a few years later.

The facility reached maximum capacity in 1955 with a population of 5,235. After a riot in 1957, it was determined that it was time to address the issue. Extensive expansions and renovations were needed to update the aging facility. Like many old buildings, it was decided that it would be too costly and too involved to make update the place.

By the early 1970s, the Southern Ohio Correctional Facility had been approved and completed. Over the next decade, prisoners were transferred from OSR to the new prison and plans to close down the antiquated facility were set into motion. OSR was officially closed down in 1984.

The building was sold by the state of Ohio to the city government of Columbus in 1995. Many ideas have been suggested as to what to do with the twenty-three acre site, including razing the old prison and turning it into a stadium and shopping center. Preservation groups stepped in to stop the demolition of the property.

The Hauntings

Prisoners weren't the only ones to die at OSR. At least two guards lost their lives in the line of duty. One guard was fatally shot by a man trying to help a prisoner escape in 1926. The other guard was beaten to death in 1932.

Could they haunt the place? Or could it be the warden or Helen? Or maybe one of the twenty-eight men who were executed here from 1885 – 1896? Could it be some of the souls who were lost to a cholera epidemic in 1849? Or perhaps some of the men who died during a 1930 fire?

We may not know exactly who is haunting the building but we know where. There have been paranormal reports in six areas: the warden's residence, the chapel, basement, West Wing shower, and cell blocks (including solitary confinement). Cells A, B, C, and D are located in the East Hall buildings. The New Hall was added in 1877. Recently, the section of the building that housed the hospital was opened to the public and there has been some paranormal activity reported in that area.

The warden's residence was in the East Administration Building. Disembodied voices believed to be male and female have been heard arguing. People have smelled roses but there are no flowers around. However, the warden's wife, Helen (who died in their residence from a gunshot wound), often kept fresh flowers in the home to make it cheerier. Roses were her favorite. EVPs recorded by ghost groups have picked up a woman's voice.

Shadowy figures have been seen in the chapel, shower, and basement. If you walk across the room towards the apparition, it will disappear. But the most haunted area is the cell blocks. Visitors have experienced everything from being pushed to being punched by an unseen presence. Female visitors and guides have had their hair pulled and their heads pushed down. Feelings of nausea and cold sensations are common, as well as an unshakable feeling of uneasiness. The sounds of footsteps, a cell door being slammed shut, and something scraping against metal has been heard. Some staff and visitors have complained that they have found it hard to breathe. Some report hearing growling.

The operations manager says that a whitish figure is often seen in the cell block area of the prison. A black mass or dark shadow is seen sometimes at the end of the cell block corridor. It is believed that the ghosts reveal themselves to visitors who appear to be afraid.

Visitor Information

The old prison is located eighty miles southwest of Cleveland. It is open to the public for a fee. The cost depends on which option you choose, such as ghost walks (usually sold out a year in advance), public and private ghost investigations, historical tours, photo tours, educational tours, etc. There are also special events, such as their Murder Mystery Dinner Theatre.

100 Reformatory Road

Mansfield, OH 44905

www.mrps.org

It takes 3 hours and fifteen minutes (175 miles) to go get from either Memphis, Tennessee or Cincinnati, Ohio to Mansfield.

Fun Quiz

1. If you decide to visit the *Queen Mary*, where would you go (city, state)?
2. There is a part of the Moon River Brewing Company that no one is allowed to go. Where is this?
3. What kind of facility was the Waverly Hills Sanatorium?
4. Name the voodoo priestess who is buried in St. Louis Cemetery and believed to one of the spirits which haunt the place.
5. What is the first *penitentiary* in the world and also one of the most expensive to build?
6. Where is the Pirates' House?
7. What is the most haunted room in Belcourt Castle?
8. Where does the spirit of "Red" reside?
9. Bizarre occult rituals were once performed where?
10. Which haunted place has 140 visible bullet holes and is the site of 26 deaths?

Answers

1. Long Beach, CA

2. The top floor were the ghost resides

3. Tuberculosis

4. Marie Laveau

5. Eastern State Pen

6. Historic District of Savannah, GA

7. Ballroom

8. Lincoln Theatre

9. Bobby Mackey's Music World

10. Birdcage Theatre

Index

TERRANCE ZEPKE
Series Reading Order
& Guide

Series List

Most Haunted Series

Terrance Talks Travel Series

Cheap Travel Series

Spookiest Series

Stop Talking Series

Carolinas for Kids Series

Ghosts of the Carolinas Series

Books & Guides for the Carolinas Series

& More Books by Terrance Zepke

≈

Introduction

Here is a list of titles by Terrance Zepke. They are presented in chronological order although they do not need to be read in any particular order.

Also included is an author bio, a personal message from Terrance, and some other information you may find helpful.

All books are available as digital and print books. They can be found on Amazon, Barnes and Noble, Kobo, Apple iBooks, GooglePlay, Smashwords, or through your favorite independent bookseller.

For more about this author and her books visit her Author Page at:

http://www.amazon.com/Terrance-Zepke/e/B000APJNIA/.

You can also connect with Terrance on Twitter **@terrancezepke** or on

www.facebook.com/terrancezepke

www.pinterest.com/terrancezepke

www.goodreads.com/terrancezepke

Sign up for weekly email notifications of the **Terrance Talks Travel** blog to be the first to learn about new episodes of her travel show, cheap travel tips, free downloadable TRAVEL REPORTS, and discover her TRIP PICK OF THE WEEK at www.terrancetalkstravel.com or sign up for her **Mostly Ghostly** blog at www.terrancezepke.com.

≈

TERRANCE TALKS TRAVEL

Podcast

You can follow her travel show, **TERRANCE TALKS TRAVEL: ÜBER ADVENTURES on** www.blogtalkradio.com/terrancetalkstravel or subscribe to it at **iTunes.**

Warning: Listening to this show could lead to a spectacular South African safari, hot-air ballooning over the Swiss Alps, Disney Adventures, and Tornado Tours!

≈

Terrance Zepke is co-host of the writing show, **A WRITER'S JOURNEY: FROM BLANK PAGE TO PUBLISHED.** All episodes can be found on **iTunes** or on **www.terrancezepke.com.**

≈

AUTHOR BIO

Terrance Zepke studied Journalism at the University of Tennessee and later received a Master's degree in Mass Communications from the University of South Carolina. She studied parapsychology at the renowned Rhine Research Center.

Zepke spends much of her time happily traveling around the world but always returns home to the Carolinas where she lives part-time in both states. She has written hundreds of articles and more than fifty books. She is the host of *Terrance Talks Travel: Über Adventures* and co-host of *A Writer's Journey: From Blank Page to Published.* Additionally, this award-winning and best-selling author has been featured in many publications and programs, such as NPR, CNN, *The Washington Post,* Associated Press, Travel with Rick Steves, Around the World, *Publishers Weekly,* World Travel & Dining with Pierre Wolfe, *San Francisco Chronicle*, Good Morning Show, *Detroit Free Press*, The Learning Channel, and The Travel Channel.

When she's not investigating haunted places, searching for pirate treasure, or climbing lighthouses, she is most likely packing for her next adventure to some far flung place, such as Reykjavik or Kwazulu Natal. Some of her favorite adventures include piranha fishing on the Amazon, shark cage diving in South Africa, hiking the Andes Mountains Inca Trail, camping in the Himalayas, dog-sledding in the Arctic Circle, and a gorilla safari in the Congo.

≈

MOST HAUNTED SERIES

A Ghost Hunter's Guide to the Most Haunted Places in America
(2012)
https://read.amazon.com/kp/embed?asin=B0085SG22O&previe
w=newtab&linkCode=kpe&ref_=cm_sw_r_kb_dp_zerQwb1AM
J0R4

A Ghost Hunter's Guide to the Most Haunted Houses in America
(2013)
https://read.amazon.com/kp/embed?asin=B00C3PUMGC&previ
ew=newtab&linkCode=kpe&ref_=cm_sw_r_kb_dp_BfrQwb1W
F1Y6T

*A Ghost Hunter's Guide to the Most Haunted Hotels & Inns in
America* (2014)
https://read.amazon.com/kp/embed?asin=B00C3PUMGC&previ
ew=newtab&linkCode=kpe

*A Ghost Hunter's Guide to the Most Haunted Historic Sites in
America* (2016)
https://www.amazon.com/Ghost-Hunters-Haunted-Historic-
America-
ebook/dp/B01LXADK90/ref=sr_1_1?s=books&ie=UTF8&qid=1
475973918&sr=1-
1&keywords=a+ghost+hunter%27s+guide+to+the+most+haunte
d+historic+sites+in+america

*The Ghost Hunter's MOST HAUNTED Box Set (3 in 1):
Discover America's Most Haunted Destinations* (2016)
https://read.amazon.com/kp/embed?asin=B01HISAAJM&previe
w=newtab&linkCode=kpe&ref_=cm_sw_r_kb_dp_ulz-
xbNKND7VT

MOST HAUNTED and SPOOKIEST Sampler Box Set:
Featuring *A GHOST HUNTER'S GUIDE TO THE MOST
HAUNTED PLACES IN AMERICA* and *SPOOKIEST
CEMETERIES* (2017)

https://read.amazon.com/kp/embed?asin=B01N17EEOM&previe
w=newtab&linkCode=kpe&ref_=cm_sw_r_kb_dp_.JFLybCTN3
QEF

≈

TERRANCE TALKS TRAVEL SERIES

Terrance Talks Travel: A Pocket Guide to South Africa (2015)
https://read.amazon.com/kp/embed?asin=B00PSTFTLI&preview
=newtab&linkCode=kpe&ref_=cm_sw_r_kb_dp_pirQwb12XZX
65

Terrance Talks Travel: A Pocket Guide to African Safaris (2015)
https://read.amazon.com/kp/embed?asin=B00PSTFZSA&previe
w=newtab&linkCode=kpe&ref_=cm_sw_r_kb_dp_jhrQwb0P8Z
87G

Terrance Talks Travel: A Pocket Guide to Adventure Travel
(2015)
https://read.amazon.com/kp/embed?asin=B00UKMAVQG&prev
iew=newtab&linkCode=kpe&ref_=cm_sw_r_kb_dp_ThrQwb1P
VVZAZ

*Terrance Talks Travel: A Pocket Guide to Florida Keys
(including Key West & The Everglades)* (2016)
http://www.amazon.com/Terrance-Talks-Travel-Including-
Everglades-
ebook/dp/B01EWHML58/ref=sr_1_1?s=books&ie=UTF8&qid=
1461897775&sr=1-
1&keywords=terrance+talks+travel%3A+a+pocket+guide+to+th
e+florida+keys

Terrance Talks Travel: The Quirky Tourist Guide to Key West
(2017)
https://www.amazon.com/Terrance-
Zepke/e/B000APJNIA/ref=sr_ntt_srch_lnk_1?qid=1485052308
&sr=8-1

Terrance Talks Travel: The Quirky Tourist Guide to Cape Town
(2017)
https://www.amazon.com/Terrance-

Zepke/e/B000APJNIA/ref=sr_ntt_srch_lnk_1?qid=1485052308&sr=8-1

Terrance Talks Travel: The Quirky Tourist Guide to Reykjavik (2017)
https://www.amazon.com/Terrance-Zepke/e/B000APJNIA/ref=sr_ntt_srch_lnk_15?qid=1488514258&sr=8-15

Terrance Talks Travel: The Quirky Tourist Guide to Charleston, South Carolina (2017)
https://www.amazon.com/Terrance-Zepke/e/B000APJNIA/ref=sr_ntt_srch_lnk_15?qid=1488514258&sr=8-15

Terrance Talks Travel: The Quirky Tourist Guide to Ushuaia (2017)
https://www.amazon.com/Terrance-Zepke/e/B000APJNIA/ref=sr_ntt_srch_lnk_15?qid=1488514258&sr=8-15

Terrance Talks Travel: The Quirky Tourist Guide to Antarctica (2017) https://www.amazon.com/Terrance-Zepke/e/B000APJNIA/ref=sr_ntt_srch_lnk_1?qid=1489092624&sr=8-1

TERRANCE TALKS TRAVEL: The Quirky Tourist Guide to Machu Picchu & Cuzco (Peru) 2017
https://read.amazon.com/kp/embed?asin=B07147HLQY&preview=newtab&linkCode=kpe&ref_=cm_sw_r_kb_dp_HmZmzb9FT5E0P

African Safari Box Set: Featuring TERRANCE TALKS
TRAVEL: *A Pocket Guide to South Africa* and *TERRANCE
TALKS TRAVEL: A Pocket Guide to African Safaris* (2017)
https://read.amazon.com/kp/embed?asin=B01MUH6VJU&preview=n
ewtab&linkCode=kpe&ref_=cm_sw_r_kb_dp_xLFLybAQKFAOB

≈

CHEAP TRAVEL SERIES

How to Cruise Cheap! (2017)

https://www.amazon.com/Cruise-Cheap-CHEAP-TRAVEL-Book-ebook/dp/B01N6NYM1N/

How to Fly Cheap! (2017)

https://www.amazon.com/How-Cheap-CHEAP-TRAVEL-Book-ebook/dp/B01N7Q81YG/

How to Travel Cheap! (2017)

https://read.amazon.com/kp/embed?asin=B01N7Q81YG&preview=newtab&linkCode=kpe&ref_=cm_sw_r_kb_dp_j78KybJVSCXDX

How to Travel FREE or Get Paid to Travel! (2017)

https://read.amazon.com/kp/embed?asin=B01N7Q81YG&preview=newtab&linkCode=kpe&ref_=cm_sw_r_kb_dp_j78KybJVSCXDX

CHEAP TRAVEL SERIES (4 IN 1) BOX SET (2017)

https://read.amazon.com/kp/embed?asin=B071ZGV1TY&preview=newtab&linkCode=kpe&ref_=cm_sw_r_kb_dp_rlZmzbSPV8KG9

SPOOKIEST SERIES

Spookiest Lighthouses (2013)
https://read.amazon.com/kp/embed?asin=B00EAAQA2S&previe
w

Spookiest Battlefields (2015)
https://read.amazon.com/kp/embed?asin=B00XUSWS3G&previ
ew=newtab&linkCode=kpe&ref_=cm_sw_r_kb_dp_okrQwb0TR
9F8M

Spookiest Cemeteries (2016)
http://www.amazon.com/Terrance-
Zepke/e/B000APJNIA/ref=sr_ntt_srch_lnk_1?qid=1457641303
&sr=8-1

Spookiest Objects (2017)
https://read.amazon.com/kp/embed?asin=B0728FMVZF&previe
w=newtab&linkCode=kpe&ref_=cm_sw_r_kb_dp_eqZmzbN217
2VR

*Spookiest Box Set (3 in 1): Discover America's Most Haunted
Destinations* (2016)
https://read.amazon.com/kp/embed?asin=B01HH2OM4I&previe
w=newtab&linkCode=kpe&ref_=cm_sw_r_kb_dp_Anz-
xbT3SDEZS

MOST HAUNTED and SPOOKIEST Sampler Box Set:
Featuring *A GHOST HUNTER'S GUIDE TO THE MOST
HAUNTED PLACES IN AMERICA* and *SPOOKIEST
CEMETERIES* (2017)

https://read.amazon.com/kp/embed?asin=B01N17EEOM&preview=n
ewtab&linkCode=kpe&ref_=cm_sw_r_kb_dp_.JFLybCTN3QEF

STOP TALKING SERIES

Stop Talking & Start Writing Your Book (2015)
https://read.amazon.com/kp/embed?asin=B012YHTIAY&previe
w=newtab&linkCode=kpe&ref_=cm_sw_r_kb_dp_qlrQwb1N7G
3YF

Stop Talking & Start Publishing Your Book (2015)
https://read.amazon.com/kp/embed?asin=B013HHV1LE&previe
w=newtab&linkCode=kpe&ref_=cm_sw_r_kb_dp_WlrQwb1F6
3MFD

Stop Talking & Start Selling Your Book (2015)
https://read.amazon.com/kp/embed?asin=B015YAO33K&previe
w=newtab&linkCode=kpe&ref_=cm_sw_r_kb_dp_ZkrQwb188J
8BE

Stop Talking & Start Writing Your Book Series (3 in 1) Box Set
(2016) https://www.amazon.com/Stop-Talking-Start-Writing-
Box-
ebook/dp/B01M58J5AZ/ref=sr_1_5?s=books&ie=UTF8&qid=1
475974073&sr=1-5&keywords=stop+talking+and+start+writing

≈

Terrance Zepke

CAROLINAS FOR KIDS SERIES

Lighthouses of the Carolinas for Kids (2009)
http://www.amazon.com/Lighthouses-Carolinas-Kids-Terrance-Zepke/dp/1561644293/ref=asap_bc?ie=UTF8

Pirates of the Carolinas for Kids (2009)
https://read.amazon.com/kp/embed?asin=B01BJ3VSWK&preview=newtab&linkCode=kpe&ref_=cm_sw_r_kb_dp_rGrXwb0XDTSTA

Ghosts of the Carolinas for Kids (2011)
https://read.amazon.com/kp/embed?asin=B01BJ3VSVQ&preview=newtab&linkCode=kpe&ref_=cm_sw_r_kb_dp_XLrXwb0E7N1AK

≈

GHOSTS OF THE CAROLINAS SERIES

Ghosts of the Carolina Coasts (1999)
http://www.amazon.com/Ghosts-Carolina-Coasts-Terrance-Zepke/dp/1561641758/ref=asap_bc?ie=UTF8

The Best Ghost Tales of South Carolina (2004)
http://www.amazon.com/Best-Ghost-Tales-South-Carolina/dp/1561643068/ref=asap_bc?ie=UTF8

Ghosts & Legends of the Carolina Coasts (2005)
https://read.amazon.com/kp/embed?asin=B01AGQJABW&preview=newtab&linkCode=kpe&ref_=cm_sw_r_kb_dp_VKrXwb1Q09794

The Best Ghost Tales of North Carolina (2006)
https://read.amazon.com/kp/embed?asin=B01BJ3VSV6&preview=newtab&linkCode=kpe&ref_=cm_sw_r_kb_dp_6IrXwb0XKT90Q

≈

Terrance Zepke

BOOKS & GUIDES FOR THE CAROLINAS SERIES

Pirates of the Carolinas (2005)
http://www.amazon.com/Pirates-Carolinas-Terrance-Zepke/dp/1561643440/ref=asap_bc?ie=UTF8

Coastal South Carolina: Welcome to the Lowcountry (2006)
http://www.amazon.com/Coastal-South-Carolina-Welcome-Lowcountry/dp/1561643483/ref=asap_bc?ie=UTF8

Coastal North Carolina: Its Enchanting Islands, Towns & Communities (2011)
http://www.amazon.com/Coastal-North-Carolina-Terrance-Zepke/dp/1561645117/ref=asap_bc?ie=UTF8

Lighthouses of the Carolinas: A Short History & Guide (2011)
https://read.amazon.com/kp/embed?asin=B01AGQJA7G&preview=newtab&linkCode=kpe&ref_=cm_sw_r_kb_dp_UHrXwb09A22P1

≈

MORE BOOKS BY TERRANCE ZEPKE

Lowcountry Voodoo: Tales, Spells & Boo Hags (2009)
https://read.amazon.com/kp/embed?asin=B018WAGUC6&previ
ew=newtab&linkCode=kpe&ref_=cm_sw_r_kb_dp_UmrQwb19
AVSYG

Ghosts of Savannah (2012)
http://www.amazon.com/Ghosts-Savannah-Terrance-
Zepke/dp/1561645303/ref=asap_bc?ie=UTF8

How to Train Any Puppy or Dog Using Three Simple Strategies
(2017)
https://www.amazon.com/Train-Puppy-Using-Simple-Strategies-
ebook/dp/B01MZ5GN2M/ref=asap_bc?ie=UTF8

*Fiction books written under a pseudonym

≈

Message from the Author

The primary purpose of this guide is to introduce you to some titles you may not have known about. Another reason for it is to let you know all the ways you can connect with me. Authors love to hear from readers. We truly appreciate you more than you'll ever know. Please feel free to send me a comment or question via the comment form found on every page on www.terrancezepke.com and www.terrancetalkstravel.com or follow me on your favorite social media. Don't forget that you can also listen to my writing podcast on iTunes, **A Writer's Journey**, or my travel show, **Terrance Talks Travel: Über Adventures** on Blog Talk Radio and iTunes. The best way to make sure you don't miss any episodes of these shows (and find a complete archive of shows), new book releases and giveaways, contests, my TRIP PICK OF THE WEEK, cheap travel tips, free downloadable ghost and travel reports, and more is to subscribe to *Terrance Talks Travel* on www.terrancetalkstravel.com or *Mostly Ghostly* on www.terrancezepke.com. If you'd like to learn more about any of my books, you can find in-depth descriptions and "look inside" options through most online booksellers. Also, please note that links to book previews have been included in SERIES section of this booklet for your convenience.

Thank you for your interest and HAPPY READING!

Terrance

Turn the page for a special preview of the latest book in Terrance Zepke's 'most haunted' series:

A GHOST HUNTER'S GUIDE TO THE MOST HAUNTED HISTORIC SITES IN AMERICA

Available from Safari Publishing

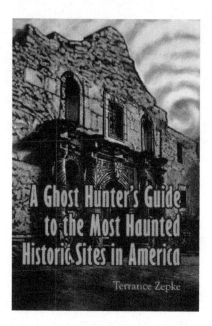

White House

FUN FACTS:

There have been many séances held in the White House as some occupants have tried to connect with its resident ghosts.

The White House has been home to every President since John Adams in 1800.

The most haunted area is the Lincoln bedroom, but there are many other haunted areas throughout the White House. The Executive Mansion includes 132 rooms, 35 bathrooms, and six levels in the residence. There are three elevators, 8 staircases, 28 fireplaces, and 412 doors.

The History

It was built from 1792 – 1800. It was set on fire by the British Army during the War of 1812. While most of the interior was destroyed, the exterior was not too badly damaged and was soon repaired.

When Teddy Roosevelt was president, he had all the offices moved to a new addition he authorized called the West Wing. The West Wing was enlarged during William Taft's presidency. He also added the Oval Office and the East Wing. Thomas Jefferson added grandiose colonnades, which connected the two wings.

Each president added his personal touches, ranging from subtle to drastic changes. Today, the White House is a complex that includes the Blair House (guest house), East Wing, Eisenhower Executive Office Building, West Wing, and main house. The main house is six stories: ground, state, second, third, and a two-story basement.

The White House is a National Heritage Site owned by the National Park Service. Here are ten fun facts about the White House (provided by the White House Historical Association):

1. George Washington is the only president never to have slept in the White House.

2. The total cost of the original structure was $232,372.

3. The White House was the largest house in the United States until after the Civil War.

4. Today, the home's square footage is about 55,000. It features six levels, eight staircases,

three elevators, 28 fireplaces and 132 rooms, including 35 bathrooms.

5. The White House grounds and garden crew consist of 13 full-time staff members, and there are five full-time chefs.

6. The nation's Executive Mansion officially became known as the White House during the administration of Theodore Roosevelt, who directed that all government correspondence use the title.

7. Benjamin Harrison brought the first Christmas tree inside in 1889.

8. The property features a tennis court, a bowling alley, a movie theater, a beauty salon, a physician's office, a florist's shop, a swimming pool and a golf putting green. Dwight Eisenhower had the first putting green installed. Richard Nixon and his wife, Pat, were avid bowlers. A jogging track was added around the driveway of the South grounds during Bill Clinton's first term.

9. The White House was designated a National Historic Landmark in 1960.

10. Each president sits for a portrait that is added to the presidential collection housed in the White House.

 The Hauntings

There are many reportedly haunted areas of the White House, but it is hard to prove or disprove these reports given that ghost investigations are not permitted. However, we do have some evidence and a "top ten" list of the most haunted areas of the White House.

Yellow Oval Room

Haunt Spot #10: Yellow Oval Room. During Lincoln's administration, this room was his personal library and one of his favorite rooms in the White House. Numerous White House employees have reportedly seen Lincoln gazing out the windows of this room. First Lady Grace Coolidge also claimed to have seen him here. First Lady Mary Todd Lincoln also reported seeing the ghosts of both Presidents Thomas Jefferson and John Tyler here.

Haunt Spot #9: The Attic. President William Henry Harrison only held office for one month before dying of pneumonia. A spirit lingers in the attic, seemingly searching for something. More than a few presidents have reported hearing noises coming from the attic over the Oval Office to their Secret Service detail. No one is ever found, but some believe the noises are attributed to the ghost of Harrison, who may feel he didn't do his duty while alive, so his spirit is serving the rest of his term—and then some!

Haunt Spot #8: Rose Garden. The Rose Garden was conceived by First Lady Dolley Madison. When First Lady Ellen Wilson requested the garden be dug out during her tenure one hundred years later, the ghost of Dolley Madison appeared in the garden. And every time workers tried to fulfill Wilson's request, her spirit appeared or made its presence known. The First Lady's plan to destroy the garden was abandoned and there were no more sightings of Dolley Madison in the Rose Garden.

Haunt Spot #7: The Basement. Isn't it always haunted? But this basement is haunted by a phantom cat. It rarely appears but when it does it is to signal a national disaster. It has appeared before the great stock market crash and Great Depression, before John F. Kennedy's assassination, and other momentous occasions.

Haunt Spot #6: Second Floor Hall. This hall is part of the residence of the first family. Lincoln has been seen in these hallways by Lady Eleanor Roosevelt, President Truman, and President Taft claims to have seen First Lady Abigail Adams disappearing through a door.

Haunt Spot #5: Second Floor Bedroom. President Johnson's daughter, Lynda, claimed she saw the ghost of Abraham Lincoln's son. Willie died in the same bedroom that Lynda was using. Ghostly screams have been heard on occasion, which some believe belong to President Grove Cleveland's wife, who gave birth in this room.

Haunt Spot #4: North Portico. A British soldier has been seen here. He is carrying a torch, presumably the spirit of a soldier who was sent here during the War of 1812 to burn the White

House. The ghost of Anne Surratt is also seen here. She was the daughter of Mary Surratt, who was hanged for her part in Lincoln's assassination. The ghost of Anne Surratt is sometimes heard pounding on the door, begging for her mother's life to be spared and sitting on the front steps on the anniversary of her mother's execution.

Haunt Spot #3: East Room. It is haunted by the ghost of Abigail Adams, who used it as her laundry room. An apparition is seen carrying a basket that resembles a vintage laundry basket. In 2002, a group of tourists witnessed this sight. The smell of laundry soap is also detected sometimes even though it has been a long time since laundry was done in this room—or since a first lady was tasked with laundry duty!

Haunt Spot #2: Rose Room. Sightings of President Andrew Johnson are seen in this room. He is heard cussing or laughing. There is an unexplainable cold spot in the room. Lincoln has been glimpsed in this room on occasion. Queen Wilhelmina of the Netherlands heard a knock at the door while she was sleeping in this room.

When she answered it, she saw Abraham Lincoln disappearing down the hallway.

Lincoln's Bedroom

Haunt Spot #1: The most haunted area in the White House is Lincoln's Bedroom. Winston Churchill refused to sleep in the bedroom again after seeing the ghost of Abraham Lincoln beside the fireplace. According to the story, Churchill had just gotten out of the bath, so he was completely naked when he saw the ghost.

Beyond those already listed as seeing Lincoln in other places, he has been spotted by Teddy Roosevelt, Herbert Hoover, and Dwight Eisenhower; First Ladies Jacquie Kennedy and Ladybird Johnson; and presidential children Susan Ford and Maureen Reagan (and her husband). Other guests have reported that lights in the bedroom turn on and off by themselves, and there are inexplicable cold spots in the room.

President Kennedy's Press Secretary James Haggerty swore he saw President Lincoln in the White House. President Bill Clinton's Press Secretary Mike McCurry must have had a ghostly encounter because he has publicly announced his belief that there are ghosts in the White House. Most modern day presidents won't admit they've witnessed anything paranormal. Perhaps they are worried about public perception. However, Hillary Clinton has stated that she has felt the spirits of all the people who have lived there and that the White House can be creepy at times.

White House séances were fairly common when Abraham Lincoln was president. Ulysses S. Grant allegedly took part in a séance and communicated with Willie Lincoln. Other unconfirmed séances include Nancy Reagan and Hillary Clinton.

There are many more ghostly encounters reported by White House staff over the years. There are also other ghosts who supposedly haunt the most famous house in America. One such ghost is David Burns. He was forced to give up his land so that the White House could be built. Some believe he never left his property. One thing is for sure. There is no disputing the fact that the White House is one of the most haunted historic sites in America.

Visitor Information

Requests for the White House tour must be submitted through your Member of Congress (https://www.whitehouse.gov/participate/tours-and-events). These self-guided tours are available in the morning Tuesday through Saturday. Tour hours are extended whenever possible as the White House schedule permits. Tours are scheduled on a first come, first served basis. You can submit a request up to six months in advance of your visit. The earlier, the better as only a limited number of spaces are available.

The White House will notify your Congressional Representative of your tour request status approximately two weeks before the tour date. Spring and summer tours fill up quickly, so make your request early. Want to see the holiday decorations? You can begin to submit your Christmas tour request in June. All tours are free of charge.

A list of the requirements and restrictions is provided on the website. A free, online **White House Tour** is also available on their website.

The **White House Garden Tour** is offered twice a year over weekends in the spring and fall.

At this time, the only way to experience a **West Wing Tour** is by invitation from the White House or through a personal connection to a White House staffer willing to lead you on an after-hours tour. But you can download an

official West Wing Tour Booklet at
https://whitehouse.gov1.info/visit/tour.html#wes
twing.

1600 Pennsylvania Ave NW, Washington, DC
20500

https://whitehouse.gov1.info/visit/tour.html

Washington, DC is one hour and forty-five
minutes from Richmond, VA (110 miles); 9
hours from Indianapolis, IN (577 miles); and 4
hours from Raleigh, NC (283 miles).

Made in the USA
Monee, IL
13 December 2020